On The Social Contract

By Jean-Jacques Rousseau

This little treatise is part of a longer work which I began years ago without realising my limitations, and long since abandoned. Of the various fragments that might have been extracted from what I wrote, this is the most considerable, and, I think, the least unworthy of being offered to the public. The rest no longer exists.

Translated By G. D. H. Cole

CONTENTS

INTRODUCTION

For the study of the great writers and thinkers of the past, historical imagination is the first necessity. Without mentally referring to the environment in which they lived, we cannot hope to penetrate below the inessential and temporary to the absolute and permanent value of their thought. Theory, no less than action, is subject to these necessities; the form in which men cast their speculations, no less than the ways in which they behave, are the result of the habits of thought and action which they find around them. Great men make, indeed, individual contributions to the knowledge of their times; but they can never transcend the age in which they live. The questions they try to answer will always be those their contemporaries are asking; their statement of fundamental problems will always be relative to the traditional statements that have been handed down to them. When they are stating what is most startlingly new, they will be most likely to put it in an old-fashioned form, and to use the inadequate ideas and formulae of tradition to express the deeper truths towards which they are feeling their way. They will be most the children of their age, when they are rising most above it.

Rousseau has suffered as much as any one from critics without a sense of history. He has been cried up and cried down by democrats and oppressors with an equal lack of understanding and imagination. His name, a hundred and fifty years after the publication of the *Social Contract*, is still a controversial watchword and a party cry. He is accepted as one of the greatest writers France has produced; but even now men are inclined, as political bias prompts them, to accept or reject his political doctrines as a whole, without sifting them or attempting to understand and discriminate. He is still revered or hated as the author who, above all others, inspired the French Revolution.

At the present day, his works possess a double significance. They are important historically, alike as giving us an insight into the mind of the eighteenth century, and for the actual influence they have had on the course of events in Europe. Certainly no other writer of the time has exercised such an influence as his. He may fairly be called the parent of the romantic movement in art, letters and life; he affected profoundly the German romantics and Goethe himself; he set the fashion of a new introspection which has permeated nineteenth century literature; he began modern educational theory; and, above all, in political thought he represents the passage from a traditional theory rooted in the Middle Ages to the modern philosophy of the State. His influence on Kant's moral philosophy and on Hegel's philosophy of Right are two sides of the same fundamental contribution to modern thought. He is, in fact, the great forerunner of German and English Idealism.

It would not be possible, in the course of a short introduction, to deal both with the positive content of Rousseau's thought and with the actual influence he has had on practical affairs. The statesmen of the French Revolution, from Robespierre downwards, were throughout profoundly affected by the study of his works. Though they seem often to have misunderstood him, they had on the whole studied him with the attention he demands. In the nineteenth century, men continued to appeal to Rousseau, without, as a rule, knowing him well or penetrating deeply into his meaning. "The *Social Contract*," says M. Dreyfus-Brisac, "is the book of all books that is most talked of and least read." But with the great revival of interest in political philosophy there has come a desire for the better understanding of Rousseau's work. He is again being studied more as a thinker and less as an ally or an opponent; there is more eagerness to sift the true from the false, and to seek in the *Social Contract* the "principles of political right," rather than the great revolutionary's *ipse dixit* in favour of some view about circumstances which he could never have; contemplated.

The *Social Contract*, then, may be regarded either as a document of the French Revolution, or as one of the greatest books dealing with political philosophy. It is in the second capacity, as a work of permanent value containing truth, that it finds a place among the world's great books. It is in that capacity also that it will be treated in this introduction. Taking it in this aspect, we have no less need of historical insight than if we came to it as historians pure and simple. To understand—its value we must grasp its limitations; when the questions it answers seem unnaturally put, we must not conclude that they are meaningless; we must see if the answer still holds when the question is put in a more up-to-date form.

First, then, we must always remember that Rousseau is writing in the eighteenth century, and for the most part in France. Neither the French monarchy nor the Genevese aristocracy loved outspoken criticism, and Rousseau had always to be very careful what he said. This may seem a curious statement to make about a man who suffered continual persecution on account of his subversive doctrines; but, although Rousseau was one of the most daring writers of his time, he was forced continually to moderate his language and, as a rule, to confine himself to generalisation instead of attacking particular abuses. Rousseau's theory has often been decried as too abstract and metaphysical. This is in many ways its great strength; but where it is excessively so, the accident of time is to blame. In the eighteenth century it was, broadly speaking, safe to generalise and unsafe to particularise. Scepticism and discontent were the prevailing temper of the intellectual classes, and a short-sighted despotism held that, as long as they were confined to these, they would do little harm. Subversive doctrines were only regarded as dangerous when they were so put as to appeal to the masses; philosophy was regarded as impotent. The intellectuals of the eighteenth century therefore generalised to their hearts' content, and as a rule suffered little for their *lèse-majesté*: Voltaire is the typical example of such generalisation. The spirit of the age favoured such methods, and it was therefore natural for Rousseau to pursue them. But his general remarks had such a way of bearing very obvious particular applications, and were so obviously inspired by a particular attitude towards the government of his day, that even philosophy became in his hands unsafe, and he was attacked for what men read between the lines of his works. It is owing to this faculty of giving his generalisations content and actuality that Rousseau has become the father of modern political philosophy. He uses the method of his time only to transcend it; out of the abstract and general he creates the concrete and universal.

Secondly, we must not forget that Rousseau's theories are to be studied in a wider historical environment. If he is the first of modern political theorists, he is also the last of a long line of Renaissance theorists, who in turn inherit and transform the concepts of mediæval thought. So many critics have spent so much wasted time in proving that Rousseau was not original only because they began by identifying originality with isolation: they studied first the *Social Contract* by itself, out of relation to earlier works, and then, having discovered that these earlier works resembled it, decided that everything it had to say was borrowed. Had they begun their study in a truly historical spirit, they would have seen that Rousseau's importance lies just in the new use he makes of old ideas, in the transition he makes from old to new in the general conception of politics. No mere innovator could have exercised such an influence or hit on so much truth. Theory makes no great leaps; it proceeds to new concepts by the adjustment and renovation of old ones. Just as theological writers on politics, from Hooker to Bossuet, make use of Biblical terminology and ideas; just as more modern writers, from Hegel to Herbert Spencer, make use of the concept of evolution, Rousseau uses the ideas and terms of the Social Contract theory. We should feel, throughout his work, his struggle to free himself from what is lifeless and outworn in that theory, while he develops out of it fruitful conceptions that go beyond its scope. A too rigid literalism in the interpretation of Rousseau's thought may easily reduce it to the possession of a merely "historical interest": if we approach it in a truly historical spirit, we shall be able to appreciate at once its temporary and its lasting value, to see how it served his contemporaries, and at the same time to disentangle from it what may be serviceable to us and for all time.

Rousseau's *Emile*, the greatest of all works on education, has already been issued in this series. In this volume are contained the most important of his political works. Of these the *Social Contract*, by far the most significant, is the latest in date. It represents the maturity of his thought, while the other works only illustrate his development. Born in 1712, he issued no work of importance till 1750; but he tells us, in the *Confessions,* that in 1743, when he was attached to the Embassy at Venice, he had already conceived the idea of a great work on *Political Institutions*, "which was to put the seal on his reputation." He seems, however, to have made little progress with this work, until in 1749 he happened to light on the announcement of a prize offered by the Academy of Dijon for an answer to the question, "Has the progress of the arts and sciences tended to the purification or to the corruption of morality?" His old ideas came thronging back, and sick at heart of the life he had been leading among the Paris *lumières*, he composed a violent and rhetorical diatribe against civilisation generally. In the following year, this work, having been awarded the prize by the Academy, was published by its author. His success was instantaneous; he became at once a famous man, the "lion" of Parisian literary circles. Refutations of his work were issued by professors, scribblers, outraged theologians and even by the King of Poland. Rousseau endeavoured to answer them all, and in the course of argument his thought developed. From 1750 to the publication of the *Social Contract* and *Emile* in 1762 he gradually evolved his views: in those twelve years he made his unique contribution to political thought.

The *Discourse on the Arts and Sciences*, the earliest of the works reproduced in this volume, is not in itself of very great importance. Rousseau has given his opinion of it in the *Confessions*. "Full of warmth and force, it is wholly without logic or order; of all my works it is the weakest in argument and the least harmonious. But whatever gifts a man may be born with, he cannot learn the art of writing in a moment." This criticism is just. The first Discourse neither is, nor attempts to be, a reasoned or a balanced production. It is the speech of an advocate, wholly one-sided and arbitrary, but so obviously and naively one-sided, that it is difficult for us to believe in its entire seriousness. At the most, it is only a rather brilliant but flimsy rhetorical effort, a sophistical improvisation, but not a serious contribution to thought. Yet it is certain that this declamation made Rousseau's name, and established his position as a great writer in Parisian circles. D'Alembert even devoted the preface of the *Encyclopædia* to a refutation. The plan of the first Discourse is essentially simple: it sets out from the badness, immorality and misery of modern nations, traces all these ills to the departure from a "natural" state, and then credits the progress of the arts and sciences with being the cause of that departure. In it, Rousseau is already in possession of his idea of "nature" as an ideal; but he has at present made no attempt to discriminate, in what is unnatural, between good and bad. He is merely using a single idea, putting it as strongly as he can, and neglecting all its limitations. The first Discourse is important not for any positive doctrine it contains, but as a key to the development of Rousseau's mind. Here we see him at the beginning of the long journey which was to lead on at last to the theory of the *Social Contract*.

In 1755 appeared the *Discourse on the Origin and Foundation of Inequality among Men*, which is the second of the works given in this volume. With this essay, Rousseau had unsuccessfully competed in 1753 for a second prize offered by the Academy of Dijon, and he now issued it prefaced by a long Dedication to the Republic of Geneva. In this work, which Voltaire, in thanking him for a presentation copy, termed his "second book against the human race," his style and his ideas have made a great advance; he is no longer content merely to push a single idea to extremes: while preserving the broad opposition between the state of nature and the state of society, which runs through all his work, he is concerned to present a rational justification of his views and to admit that a little at any rate may be said on the other side. Moreover, the idea of "nature" has already undergone a great development; it is no longer an empty opposition to the evils of society; it possesses a positive content. Thus half the *Discourse on Inequality* is occupied by an imaginary description of the state of nature, in which man is shown with ideas limited within the narrowest range, with little need of his fellows, and little care beyond provision for the necessities of the moment. Rousseau declares explicitly that he does not suppose the "state of nature" ever to have existed: it is a pure "idea of reason," a working concept reached by abstraction from the "state of society." The "natural man," as opposed to "man's man," is man stripped of all that society confers upon him, a creature formed by a process of abstraction, and never intended for a historical portrait. The conclusion of the Discourse favours not this purely abstract being, but a state of savagery intermediate between the "natural" and the "social" conditions, in which men may preserve the simplicity and the advantages of nature and at the same time secure the rude comforts and assurances of early society. In one of the long notes appended to the Discourse, Rousseau further explains his position. He does not wish, he says, that modern corrupt society should return to a state of nature: corruption has gone too far for that; he only desires now that men should palliate, by wiser use of the fatal arts, the mistake of their introduction. He recognises society as inevitable and is already feeling his way towards a justification of it. The second Discourse represents a second stage in his political thought: the opposition between the state of nature and the state of society is still presented in naked contrast; but the picture of the former has already filled out, and it only remains for Rousseau to take a nearer view of the fundamental implications of the state of society for his thought to reach maturity.

Rousseau is often blamed, by modern critics, for pursuing in the Discourses a method apparently that of history, but in reality wholly unhistorical. But it must be remembered that he himself lays no stress on the historical aspect of his work; he gives himself out as constructing a purely ideal picture, and not as depicting any actual stages in human history. The use of false historical concepts is characteristic of the seventeenth and eighteenth centuries, and Rousseau is more to be congratulated on having escaped from giving them too much importance than criticised for employing them at all.

It is doubtful whether the *Discourse on Political Economy,* first printed in the great *Encyclopædia* in 1755, was composed before or after the *Discourse on Inequality.* At first sight the former seems to be far more in the manner of the *Social Contract* and to contain views belonging essentially to Rousseau's constructive period. It would not, however, be safe to conclude from this that its date is really later. The *Discourse on Inequality* still has about it much of the rhetorical looseness of the prize essay; it aims not so much at close reasoning as at effective and popular presentation of a case. But, by reading between the lines, an attentive student can detect in it a great deal of the positive doctrine afterwards incorporated in the *Social Contract.* Especially in the closing section, which lays down the plan of a general treatment of the fundamental questions of politics, we are already to some extent in the atmosphere of the later works. It is indeed almost certain that Rousseau never attempted to put into either of the first two Discourses any of the positive content of his political theory. They were intended, not as final expositions of his point of view, but as partial and preliminary studies, in which his aim was far more destructive than constructive. It is clear that in first conceiving the plan of a work on *Political Institutions*, Rousseau cannot have meant to regard all society as in essence bad. It is indeed evident that he meant, from the first, to study human society and institutions in their rational aspect, and that he was rather diverted from his main purpose by the Academy of Dijon's competition than first induced by it to think about political questions. It need, therefore, cause no surprise that a work probably written before the *Discourse on Inequality* should contain the germs of the theory given in full in the *Social Contract.* The *Discourse on Political Economy* is important as giving the first sketch of the theory of the "General Will." It will readily be seen that Rousseau does not mean by "political economy" exactly what we mean nowadays. He begins with a discussion of the fundamental nature of the State, and the possibility of reconciling its existence with human liberty, and goes on with an admirable short study of the principles of taxation. He is thinking throughout of "political" in the sense of "public" economy, of the State as the public financier, and not of the conditions governing industry. He conceives the State as a body aiming at the well-being of all its members and subordinates all his views of taxation to that end. He who has only necessaries should not be taxed at all; superfluities should be supertaxed; there should be heavy imposts on every sort of luxury. The first part of the article is still more interesting. Rousseau begins by demolishing the exaggerated parallel so often drawn between the State and the family; he shows that the State is not, and cannot be, patriarchal in nature, and goes on to lay down his view that its real being consists in the General Will of its members. The essential features of the *Social Contract* are present in this Discourse almost as if they were commonplaces, certainly not as if they were new discoveries on which the author had just hit by some happy inspiration. There is every temptation, after reading the *Political Economy*, to suppose that Rousseau's political ideas really reached maturity far earlier than has generally been allowed.

The *Social Contract* finally appeared, along with *Emile*, in 1762. This year, therefore, represents in every respect the culmination of Rousseau's career. Henceforth, he was to write only controversial and confessional works; his theories were now developed, and, simultaneously, he gave to the world his views on the fundamental problems of politics and education. It is now time to ask what Rousseau's system, in its maturity, finally amounted to The *Social Contract* contains practically the whole of his constructive political theory; it requires to be read, for full understanding, in connection with his other works, especially *Emile* and the *Letters on the Mount* (1764), but in the main it is self-contained and complete. The title sufficiently defines its scope. It is called *The Social Contract or Principles of Political Right*, and the second title explains the first. Rousseau's object is not to deal, in a general way, like Montesquieu, with the actual institutions of existing States, but to lay down the essential principles which must form the basis of every legitimate society. Rousseau himself, in the fifth book of the *Emile*, has stated the difference clearly. "Montesquieu," he says, "did not intend to treat of the principles of political right; he was content to treat of the positive right (or law) of established governments; and no two studies could be more different than these." Rousseau then conceives his object as being something very different from that of the *Spirit of the Laws*, and it is a wilful error to misconstrue his purpose. When he remarks that "the facts," the actual history of political societies, "do not concern him," he is not contemptuous of facts; he is merely asserting the sure principle that a fact can in no case give rise to a right. His desire is to establish society on a basis of pure right, so as at once to disprove his attack on society generally and to reinforce his criticism of existing societies.

Round this point centres the whole dispute about the methods proper to political theory. There are, broadly speaking, two schools of political theorists, if we set aside the psychologists. One school, by collecting facts, aims at reaching broad generalisations about what actually happens in human societies! the other tries to penetrate to the universal principles at the root of all human combination. For the latter purpose facts may be useful, but in themselves they can prove nothing. The question is not one of fact, but one of right.

Rousseau belongs essentially to this philosophical school. He is not, as his less philosophic critics seem to suppose, a purely abstract thinker generalising from imaginary historical instances; he is a concrete thinker trying to get beyond they inessential and changing to the permanent and invariable basis of human society. Like Green, he is in search of the principle of political obligation, and beside this quest all others fall into their place as secondary and derivative. It is required to find a form of association able to defend and protect with the whole common force the person and goods of every associate, and of such a nature, that each, uniting himself with all, may still obey only himself, and remain as free as before. This is the fundamental problem of which the *Social Contract* provides the solution. The problem of political obligation is seen as including all other political problems, which fall into place in a system based upon it. How, Rousseau asks, can the will of the State help being for me a merely external will, imposing itself upon my own? How can the existence of the State be reconciled with human freedom? How can man, who is born free, rightly come to be everywhere in chains?

No-one could help understanding the central problem of the *Social Contract* immediately, were it not that its doctrines often seem to be strangely formulated. We have seen that this strangeness is due to Rousseau's historical position, to his use of the political concepts current in his own age, and to his natural tendency to build on the foundations laid by his predecessors. There are a great many people whose idea of Rousseau consists solely of the first words of the opening chapter of the *Social Contract*, "Man is born free, and everywhere he is in chains." But, they tell you, man is not born free, even if he is everywhere in chains. Thus at the very outset we are faced with the great difficulty in appreciating Rousseau. When we should naturally say "man ought to be free," or perhaps "man is born for freedom," he prefers to say "man is born free," by which he means exactly the same thing. There is doubtless, in his way of putting it, an appeal to a "golden age"; but this golden age is admittedly as imaginary as the freedom to which men are born is bound, for most of them, to be. Elsewhere Rousseau puts the point much as we might put it ourselves. "Nothing is more certain than that every man born in slavery is born for slavery.... But if there are slaves by nature, it is because there have been slaves against nature" (*Social Contract*, Book I, chap. ii).

We have seen that the contrast between the "state of nature" and the "state of society" runs through all Rousseau's work. The *Emile* is a plea for "natural" education; the Discourses are a plea for a "naturalisation" of society; the *New Héloïse* is the romantic's appeal for more "nature" in human relationships. What then is the position of this contrast in Rousseau's mature political thought? It is clear that the position is not merely that of the Discourses. In them, he envisaged only the faults of actual societies; now, he is concerned with the possibility of a rational society. His aim is to justify the change from "nature" to "society," although it has left men in chains. He is in search of the true society, which leaves men "as free as before." Altogether, the space occupied by the idea of nature in the *Social Contract* is very small. It is used of necessity in the controversial chapters, in which Rousseau is refuting false theories of social obligation; but when once he has brushed aside the false prophets, he lets the idea of nature go with them, and concerns himself solely with giving society the rational sanction he has promised. It becomes clear that, in political matters at any rate, the "state of nature" is for him only a term of controversy. He has in effect abandoned, in so far as he ever held it, the theory of a human golden age; and where, as in the *Emile*, he makes use of the idea of nature, it is broadened and deepened out of all recognition. Despite many passages in which the old terminology cleaves to him, he means by "nature" in this period not the original state of a thing, nor even its reduction to the simplest terms: he is passing over to the conception of "nature" as identical with the full development of capacity, with the higher! idea of human freedom. This view may be seen in germ even in the *Discourse on Inequality*, where, distinguishing self-respect (*amour de soi*) from egoism (*amour-propre*), Rousseau makes the former, the property of the "natural" man, consist not in the desire for self-aggrandisement, but in the seeking of satisfaction for reasonable desire accompanied by benevolence; whereas egoism is the preference of our own interests to those of others, self-respect merely puts us on an equal footing with our fellows. It is true that in the Discourse Rousseau is pleading against the development of many human faculties; but he is equally advocating the fullest development of those he regards as "natural," by which he means merely "good." The "state of society," as envisaged in the *Social Contract*, is no longer in contradiction to the "state of nature" upheld in the *Emile*, where indeed the social environment is of the greatest importance, and, though the pupil is screened from it, he is none the less being trained for it. Indeed the views given in the *Social Contract* are summarised in the fifth book of the *Emile*, and by this summary the essential unity of Rousseau's system is emphasised.

Rousseau's object, then, in the first words of the *Social Contract*, "is to inquire if, in the civil order, there can be any sure and certain, rule of administration, taking men as they are and laws as they might be." Montesquieu took laws as they were, and saw what sort of men they made: Rousseau, founding his whole system on human freedom, takes man as the basis, and regards him as giving himself what laws he pleases. He takes his stand on the nature of human freedom: on this he bases his whole system, making the will of the members the sole basis of every society.

In working out his theory, Rousseau makes use throughout of three general and, to some extent, alternative conceptions. These are the Social Contract, Sovereignty and the General Will. We shall now have to examine each of these in turn.

The Social Contract theory is as old as the sophists of Greece (see Plato, *Republic*, Book II and the *Gorgias*), and as I elusive. It has been adapted to the most opposite points of view, and used, in different forms, on both sides of every question to which it could conceivably be applied. It is frequent in mediæval writers, a commonplace with the theorists of the Renaissance, and in the eighteenth century already nearing its fall before a wider conception. It would be a long, as well as a thankless, task to trace its history over again: it may be followed best in D. G. Ritchie's admirable essay on it in *Darwin and Hegel and Other Studies*. For us, it is important only to regard it in its most general aspect, before studying the special use made of it by Rousseau. Obviously, in one form or another, it is a theory very easily arrived at. Wherever any form of government apart from the merest tyranny exists, reflection on the basis of the State cannot but lead to the notion that, in one sense or another, it is based on the consent, tacit or expressed, past or present, of its members. In this alone, the greater part of the Social Contract theory is already latent. Add the desire to find actual justification for a theory in facts, and, especially in an age possessed only of the haziest historical sense, this doctrine of consent will inevitably be given a historical setting. If in addition there is a tendency to regard society as something unnatural to humanity, the tendency will become irresistible. By writers of almost all schools, the State will be represented as having arisen, in some remote age, out of a compact or, in more legal phrase, contract between two or more parties. The only class that will be able to resist the doctrine is that which maintains the divine right of kings, and holds that all existing governments were imposed on the people by the direct interposition of God. All who are not prepared to maintain that will be partisans of some form or other of the Social Contract theory.

It is, therefore, not surprising that we find among its advocates writers of the most opposite points of view. Barely stated, it is a mere formula, which may be filled in with any content from absolutism to pure republicanism. And, in the hands of some at least of its supporters, it turns out to be a weapon that cuts both ways. We shall be in a better position to judge of its usefulness when we have seen its chief varieties at work.

All Social Contract theories that are at all definite fall under one or other of two heads. They represent society as based on an original contract either between the people and the government, or between all the individuals composing the State. Historically, modern theory passes from the first to the second of these forms.

The doctrine that society is founded on a contract between the people and the government is of mediæval origin. It was often supported by references to the Old

Testament, which contains a similar view in an unreflective form. It is found in most of the great political writers of the sixteenth century; in Buchanan, and in the writings of James I: it persists into the seventeenth in the works of Grotius and Puffendorf. Grotius is sometimes held to have stated the theory so as to admit both forms of contract; but it is clear that he is only thinking of the first form as admitting democratic as well as monarchical government. We find it put very clearly by the Convention Parliament of 1688, which accuses James II of having "endeavoured to subvert the constitution of the kingdom by breaking the original contract between king and people." While Hobbes, on the side of the royalists, is maintaining the contract theory in its second form, the Parliamentarian Algernon Sidney adheres to the idea of a contract between the people and the government.

In this form, the theory clearly admits of opposite interpretations. It may be held that the people, having given itself up once for all to its rulers, has nothing more to ask of them, and is bound to submit to any usage they may choose to inflict. This, however, is not the implication most usually drawn from it. The theory, in this form, originated with theologians who were also lawyers. Their view of a contract implied mutual obligations; they regarded the ruler as bound, by its terms, to govern constitutionally. The old idea that a king must not violate the sacred customs of the realm passes easily into the doctrine that he must not violate the terms of the original contract between himself and his people. Just as in the days of the Norman kings, every appeal on the part of the people for more liberties was couched in the form of a demand that the customs of the "good old times" of Edward the Confessor should be respected, so in the seventeenth century every act of popular assertion or resistance was stated as an appeal to the king not to violate the contract. The demand was a good popular cry, and it seemed to have the theorists behind it. Rousseau gives his refutation of this view, which he had, in the *Discourse on Inequality*, maintained in passing, in the sixteenth chapter of the third book of the *Social Contract*. (See also Book I, chap. iv, init.) His attack is really concerned also with the theory of Hobbes, which in some respects resembles, as we shall see, this first view; but, in form at least, it is directed against this form of contract. It will be possible to examine it more closely, when the second view has been considered.

The second view, which may be called the Social Contract theory proper, regards society as originating in, or based on, an agreement between the individuals composing it. It seems to be found first, rather vaguely, in Richard Hooker's *Ecclesiastical Polity*, from which Locke largely borrowed: and it reappears, in varying forms, in Milton's *Tenure of Kings and Magistrates*, in Hobbes's *Leviathan*, in Locke's *Treatises on Civil Government*, and in Rousseau. The best-known instance of its actual use is by the Pilgrim Fathers on the *Mayflower* in 1620, in whose declaration occurs the phrase, "We do solemnly and mutually, in the presence of God and of one another, covenant and combine ourselves together into a civil body politic." The natural implication of this view would seem to be the corollary of complete popular Sovereignty which Rousseau draws. But before Rousseau's time it had been used to support views as diverse as those which rested on the first form. We saw that, in Grotius's great work, *De Jure Belli et Pacis*, it was already possible to doubt which of the two theories was being advocated. The first theory was, historically, a means of popular protest against royal aggression. As soon as popular government was taken into account, the act of contract between people and government became in effect merely a contract between the individuals composing the society, and readily passed over into the second form.

The second theory, in its ordinary form, expresses only the view that the people is everywhere Sovereign, and that, in the phrase of Milton's treatise, "the power of kings and magistrates is only derivative." Before, however, this view had been worked up into a philosophical theory, it had already been used by Hobbes to support precisely opposite principles. Hobbes agrees that the original contract is one between all the individuals composing the State, and that the government is no party to it; but he regards the people as agreeing, not merely to form a State, but to invest a certain person or certain persons with the government of it. He agrees that the people is naturally supreme, but regards it as alienating its Sovereignty by the contract itself, and delegating its power, wholly and for ever, to the government. As soon, therefore, as the State is set up, the government becomes for Hobbes the Sovereign; there is no more question of popular Sovereignty, but only of passive obedience: the people is bound, by the contract, to obey its ruler, no matter whether he governs well or ill. It has alienated all its rights to the Sovereign, who is, therefore, absolute master. Hobbes, living in a time of civil wars, regards the worst government as better than anarchy, and is, therefore, at pains to find arguments in support of any form of absolutism. It is easy to pick holes in this system, and to see into what difficulties a conscientious Hobbist might be led by a revolution. For as soon as the revolutionaries get the upper hand, he will have to sacrifice one of his principles: he will have to side against either the actual or the legitimate Sovereign. It is easy also to see that alienation of liberty, even if possible for an individual, which Rousseau denies, cannot bind his posterity. But, with all its faults, the view of Hobbes is on the whole admirably, if ruthlessly, logical, and to it Rousseau owes a great deal.

The special shape given to the second Social Contract theory by Hobbes looks, at first sight, much like a combination, into a single act, of both the contracts. This, however, is not the view he adopts. The theory of a contract between government and people had, as we have seen, been used mainly as a support for popular liberties, a means of assertion against the government. Hobbes, whose whole aim is to make his government Sovereign, can only do this by leaving the government outside the contract: he thus avoids the necessity of submitting it to any obligation whatsoever, and leaves it absolute and irresponsible. He secures, in fact, not merely a State which has unbounded rights against the individual, but a determinate authority with the right to enforce those rights. His theory is not merely Statism (*étatisme*); it is pure despotism.

It is clear that, if such a theory is to be upheld, it can stand only by the view, which Hobbes shares with Grotius, that a man can alienate not merely his own liberty, but also that of his descendants, and that, consequently, a people as a whole can do the same. This is the point at which both Locke and Rousseau attack it. Locke, whose aim is largely to justify the Revolution of 1688, makes government depend, not merely at its institution, but always, on the consent of the governed, and regards all rulers as liable to be displaced if they govern tyrannically. He omits, however, to provide any machinery short of revolution for the expression of popular opinion, and, on the whole, seems to regard the popular consent as something essentially tacit and assumed. He regards the State as existing mainly to protect life and property, and is, in all his assertions of popular rights, so cautious as to reduce them almost to nothing. It is not till we come to Rousseau that the second form of the contract theory is stated in its purest and most logical form.

Rousseau sees clearly the necessity, if popular consent in government is to be more than a name, of giving it some constitutional means of expression. For Locke's theory of tacit consent, he substitutes an active agreement periodically renewed. He looks back with admiration to the city-states of ancient Greece and, in his own day, reserves his admiration for the Swiss free cities, Berne and, above all, Geneva, his native place. Seeing in the Europe of his day no case in which representative government was working at all democratically, he was unable to conceive that means might be found of giving effect to this active agreement in a nation-state; he therefore held that self-government was impossible except for a city. He wished to break up the nation-states of Europe, and create instead federative leagues of independent city-states.

It matters, however, comparatively little, for the appreciation of Rousseau's political theory in general, that he failed to become the theorist of the modern State. By taking the State, which must have, in essentials, everywhere the same basis, at its simplest, he was able, far better than his predecessors, to bring out the real nature of the "social tie," an alternative name which he often uses for the Social Contract. His doctrine I of the underlying principle of political obligation is that of all great modern writers, from Kant to Mr. Bosanquet. This fundamental unity has been obscured only because critics have failed to put the Social Contract theory in its proper place in Rousseau's system.

This theory was, we have seen, a commonplace. The amount of historical authenticity assigned to the contract almost universally presupposed varied enormously. Generally, the weaker a writer's rational basis, the more he appealed to history—and invented it. It was, therefore, almost inevitable that Rousseau should cast his theory into the contractual form. There were, indeed, writers of his time who laughed at the contract, but they were not writers who constructed a general system of political philosophy. From Cromwell to Montesquieu and Bentham, it was the practically minded man, impatient of unactual hypotheses, who refused to accept the idea of contract. The theorists were as unanimous in its favour as the Victorians were in favour of the "organic" theory. But we, criticising them in the light of later events, are in a better position for estimating the position the Social Contract really took in their political system. We see that Locke's doctrine of tacit consent made popular control so unreal that he was forced, if the State was to have any hold, to make his contract historical and actual, binding posterity for all time, and that he was also led to admit a quasi-contract between people and government, as a second vindication of popular liberties. Rousseau, on the other hand, bases no vital argument on the historical nature of the contract, in which, indeed, he clearly does not believe. "How," he asks, "did this change [from nature to society] come about?" And he answers that he does not know. Moreover, his aim is to find "a sure and legitimate rule of administration, taking men as they are and laws as they might be"; that is to say, his Social Contract is something which will be found at work in every legitimate society, but which will be in abeyance in all forms of despotism. He clearly means by it no more and no less than the fundamental principle of political association, the basis of the unity which enables us, in the State, to realise political liberty by giving up lawlessness and license. The presentation of this doctrine in the quasi-historical form of the Social Contract theory is due to the accident of the time and place in which Rousseau wrote. At the same time, the importance of the conception is best to be seen in the hard death it dies. Though no-one, for a hundred years or so, has thought of regarding it as historical, it has been found so hard to secure any other phrase explaining as well or better the basis of political union that, to this day, the phraseology of the contract theory largely persists. A conception so vital cannot have been barren.

It is indeed, in Rousseau's own thought, only one of the three different ways in which the basis of political union is stated, according to the preoccupation of his mind. When he is thinking quasi-historically, he describes his doctrine as that of the Social Contract. Modern anthropology, in its attempts to explain the complex by means of the simple, often strays further from the straight paths of history and reason. In a semi-legal aspect, using the terminology, if not the standpoint, of jurisprudence, he restates the same doctrine in the form of popular Sovereignty. This use tends continually to pass over into the more philosophical form which comes third. "Sovereignty is the exercise of the general will." Philosophically, Rousseau's doctrine finds its expression in the view that the State is based not on any original convention, not on, any determinate power, but on the living and sustaining rational will of its members. We have now to examine first Sovereignty and then the General Will, which is ultimately Rousseau's guiding conception.

Sovereignty is, first and foremost, a legal term, and it has often been held that its use in political philosophy merely leads to confusion. In jurisprudence, we are told, it has the perfectly plain meaning given to it in Austin's famous definition. The Sovereign is "a *determinate* human superior, *not* in a habit of obedience to a like superior, but receiving *habitual* obedience from the *bulk* of a given society." Where Sovereignty is placed is, on this view, a question purely of fact, and never of right. We have only to seek out the determinate human superior in a given society, and we shall have the Sovereign. In answer to this theory, it is not enough, though it is a valuable point, to show that such a determinate superior is rarely to be found. Where, for instance, is the Sovereign of England or of the British Empire? Is it the King, who is called the Sovereign? Or is it the Parliament, which is the legislature (for Austin's Sovereign is regarded as the source of law)? Or is it the electorate, or the whole mass of the population, with or without the right of voting? Clearly all these exercise a certain influence in the making of laws. Or finally, is it now the Cabinet? For Austin, one of these bodies would be ruled out as indeterminate (the mass of the population) and another as responsible (the Cabinet). But are we to regard the House of Commons or those who elect it as forming part of the Sovereign? The search for a determinate Sovereign may be a valuable legal conception; but it has evidently nothing to do with political theory.

It is, therefore, essential to distinguish between the legal Sovereign of jurisprudence, and the political Sovereign of political science and philosophy. Even so, it does not at once become clear what this political Sovereign may be. Is it the body or bodies of persons in whom political power in a State actually resides? Is it merely the complex of actual institutions regarded as embodying the will of the society? This would leave us still in the realm of mere fact, outside both right and philosophy. The Sovereign, in the philosophical sense, is neither the nominal Sovereign, nor the legal Sovereign, nor the political Sovereign of fact and common sense: it is the consequence of the fundamental bond of union, the restatement of the doctrine of Social Contract, the foreshadowing of that of General Will. The Sovereign is that body in the State in which political *power ought* always to reside, and in which the *right* to such power *does* always reside.

The idea at the back of the philosophical conception of Sovereignty is, therefore, essentially the same as that we found to underlie the Social Contract theory. It is the view that the people, whether it can alienate its right or not, is the ultimate director of its own destinies, the final power from which there is no appeal. In a sense, this is recognised even by Hobbes, who makes the power of his absolute Sovereign, the predecessor of Austin's "determinate human superior," issue first of all from the Social Contract, which is essentially a popular act. The difference between Hobbes and Rousseau on this point is solely that Rousseau regards as inalienable a supreme power which Hobbes makes the people alienate in its first corporate action. That is to say, Hobbes in fact accepts the theory of popular supremacy in name only to destroy it in fact; Rousseau asserts the theory in its only logical form, and is under no temptation to evade it by means of false historical assumptions. In Locke, a distinction is already drawn between the legal and the actual Sovereign, which Locke calls "supreme power"; Rousseau unites the absolute Sovereignty of Hobbes and the "popular consent" of Locke into the philosophic doctrine of popular Sovereignty, which has since been the established form of the theory. His final view represents a return from the perversions of Hobbes to a doctrine already familiar to mediæval and Renaissance writers; but it is not merely a return. In its passage the view has fallen into its place in a complete system of political philosophy.

In a second important respect Rousseau differentiates himself from Hobbes. For Hobbes, the Sovereign is identical with the government. He is so hot for absolutism largely because he regards revolution, the overthrow of the existing government, as at the same time the dissolution of the body politic, and a return to complete anarchy or to the "state of nature." Rousseau and, to some extent, Locke meet this view by sharp division between the supreme power and the government. For Rousseau, they are so clearly distinct that even a completely democratic government is not at the same time the Sovereign; its members are sovereign only in a different capacity and as a different corporate body, just as two different societies may exist for different purposes with exactly the same members. Pure democracy, however, the government of the State by all the people in every detail, is not, as Rousseau says, a possible human institution. All governments are really *mixed* in character; and what we call a democracy is only a more or less democratic government. Government, therefore, will always be to some extent in the hands of selected persons. Sovereignty, on the other hand, is in his view absolute, inalienable, indivisible, and indestructible. It cannot be limited, abandoned, shared or destroyed. It is an essential part of all social life that the right to control the destinies of the State belongs in the last resort to the whole people. There clearly must in the end be somewhere in the society an ultimate court of appeal, whether determinate or not; but, unless Sovereignty is distinguished from government, the government, passing under the name of Sovereign, will inevitably be regarded as absolute. The only way to avoid the conclusions of Hobbes is, therefore, to establish a clear separation between them.

Rousseau tries to do this by an adaptation of the doctrine of the "three powers." But instead of three independent powers sharing the supreme authority, he gives only two, and makes one of these wholly dependent on the other. He substitutes for the co-ordination of the legislative, the executive, and the judicial authorities, a system in which the legislative power, or Sovereign, is always supreme, the executive, or government, always secondary and derivative, and the judicial power merely a function of government. This division he makes, naturally, one of *will* and *power*. The government is merely to carry out the decrees, or acts of will, of the Sovereign people. Just as the human will transfers a command to its members for execution, so the body politic may give its decisions force by setting up authority which, like the brain, may command its members. In delegating the power necessary for the execution of its will, it is abandoning none of its supreme authority. It remains Sovereign, and can at any moment recall the grants it has made. Government, therefore, exists only at the Sovereign's pleasure, and is always revocable by the sovereign will.

It will be seen, when we come to discuss the nature of the General Will, that this doctrine really contains the most valuable part of Rousseau's theory. Here, we are concerned rather with its limitations. The distinction between legislative and executive functions is in practice very hard to draw. In Rousseau's case, it is further complicated by the presence of a second distinction. The legislative power, the Sovereign, is concerned only with what is general, the executive only with what is particular. This distinction, the full force of which can only be seen in connection with the General Will, means roughly that a matter is general when it concerns the whole community equally, and makes no mention of any particular class; as soon as it refers to any class or person, it becomes particular, and can no longer form the subject matter of an act of Sovereignty. However just this distinction may seem in the abstract, it is clear that its effect is to place all the power in the hands of the executive: modern legislation is almost always concerned with particular classes and interests. It is not, therefore, a long step from the view of Rousseau to the modern theory of democratic government, in which the people has little power beyond that of removing its rulers if they displease it. As long, however, as we confine our view to the city-state of which Rousseau is thinking, his distinction is capable of preserving for the people a greater actual exercise of will. A city can often generalise where a nation must particularise.

It is in the third book of the *Social Contract*, where Rousseau is discussing the problem of government, that it is most essential to remember that his discussion has in view mainly the city-state and not the nation. Broadly put, his principle of government is that democracy is possible only in small States, aristocracy in those of medium extent, and monarchy in great States (Book III, chap. iii). In considering this view, we have to take into account two things. First, he rejects representative government; will being, in his theory, inalienable, representative Sovereignty is impossible. But, as he regards all general acts as functions of Sovereignty, this means that no general act can be within the competence of a representative assembly. In judging this theory, we must take into account all the circumstances of Rousseau's time. France, Geneva and England were the three States he took most into account. In France, representative government was practically non-existent; in Geneva, it was only partially necessary; in England, it was a mockery, used to support a corrupt oligarchy against a debased monarchy. Rousseau may well be pardoned for not taking the ordinary modern view of it. Nor indeed is it, even in the modern world, so satisfactory an instrument of the popular will that we can afford wholly to discard his criticism. It is one of the problems of the day to find some means of securing effective popular control over a weakened Parliament and a despotic Cabinet.

The second factor is the immense development of local government. It seemed to Rousseau that, in the nation-state, all authority must necessarily pass, as it had in France, to the central power. Devolution was hardly dreamed of; and Rousseau saw the only means of securing effective popular government in a federal system, starting from the small unit as Sovereign. The nineteenth century has proved the falsehood of much of his theory of government; but there are still many wise comments and fruitful suggestions to be found in the third book of the *Social Contract* and in the treatise on the *Government of Poland*, as well as in his adaptation and criticism of the *Polysynodie* of the Abbé de Saint-Pierre, a scheme of local government for France, born out of its due time.

The point in Rousseau's theory of Sovereignty that offers most difficulty is his view (Book II, chap. vii) that, for every State, a *Legislator* is necessary. We shall understand the section only by realising that the legislator is, in fact, in Rousseau's system, the spirit of institutions personified; his place, in a developed society, is taken by the whole complex of social custom, organisation and tradition that has grown up with the State. This is made clearer by the fact that the legislator is not to exercise legislative power; he is merely to submit his suggestions for popular approval. Thus Rousseau recognises that, in the case of institutions and traditions as elsewhere, will, and not force, is the basis of the State.

This may be seen in his treatment of law as a whole (Book II, chap. vi), which deserves very careful attention. He defines laws as "acts of the general will," and, agreeing with Montesquieu in making law the "condition of civil association," goes beyond him only in tracing it more definitely to its origin in an act of will. The Social Contract renders law necessary, and at the same time makes it quite clear that laws can proceed only from the body of citizens who have constituted the State. "Doubtless," says Rousseau, "there is a universal justice emanating from reason alone; but this justice, to be admitted among us, must be mutual. Humbly speaking, in default of natural sanctions, the laws of justice are ineffective among men." Of the law which set up among men this reign of mutual justice the General Will is the source.

We thus come at last to the General Will, the most disputed, and certainly the most fundamental, of all Rousseau's political concepts. No critic of the *Social Contract* has found it easy to say either what precisely its author meant by it, or what is its final value for political philosophy. The difficulty is increased because Rousseau himself sometimes halts in the sense which he assigns to it, and even seems to suggest by it two different ideas. Of its broad meaning, however, there can be no doubt. The effect of the Social Contract is the creation of a new individual. When it has taken place, "at once, in place of the individual personality of each contracting party, the act of association creates a moral and collective body, composed of as many members as the assembly contains voters, and receiving from the act its unity, its common identity (*moi commun*), its life and its will" (Book I, chap. vi). The same doctrine had been stated earlier, in the *Political Economy*, without the historical setting. "The body politic is also a moral being, possessed of a will, and this general will, which tends always to the preservation and welfare of the whole and of every part, and is the source of the laws, constitutes for all the members of the State, in their relations to one another and to it, the rule of what is just or unjust." It will be seen at once that the second statement, which could easily be fortified by others from the *Social Contract*, says more than the first. It is not apparent that the common will, created by the institution of society, need "tend always to the welfare of the whole." Is not the common will at least as fallible as the will of a single individual? May it not equally be led away from its true interests to the pursuit of pleasure or of something which is really harmful to it? And, if the whole society may vote what conduces to the momentary pleasure of all the members and at the same time to the lasting damage of the State as a whole, is it not still more likely that some of the members will try to secure their private interests in opposition to those of the whole and of others? All these questions, and others like them, have been asked by critics of the conception of the General Will.

Two main points are involved, to one of which Rousseau gives a clear and definite answer. "There is often," he says, "a great deal of difference between the *will of all* and the *general will*; the latter takes account only of the common interest, while the former takes private interest into account, and is no more than a sum of particular wills." "The agreement of all interests is formed by opposition to that of each" (Book II, chap. iii). It is indeed possible for a citizen, when an issue is presented to him, to vote not for the good of the State, but for his own good; but, in such a case, his vote, from the point of view of the General Will, is merely negligible. But "does it follow that the general will is exterminated or corrupted? Not at all: it is always constant, unalterable, and pure; but it is subordinated to other wills which encroach upon its sphere.... The fault [each man] commits [in detaching his interest from the common interest] is that of changing the state of the question, and answering something different from what he is asked. Instead of saying by his vote 'It is to the advantage of the State,' he says, 'It is to the advantage of this or that man or party that this or that view should prevail.' Thus the law of public order in assemblies is not so much to maintain in them the general will as to secure that the question be always put to it, and the answer always given by it" (Book IV, chap. i). These passages, with many others that may be found in the text, make it quite clear that by the General Will Rousseau means something quite distinct from the Will of All, with which it should never have been confused. The only excuse for such confusion lies in his view that when, *in a city-state*, all particular associations are avoided, votes guided by individual self-interest will always cancel one another, so that majority voting will always result in the General Will. This is clearly not the case, and in this respect we may charge him with pushing the democratic argument too far. The point, however, can be better dealt with at a later stage. Rousseau makes no pretence that the mere voice of a majority is infallible; he only says, at the most, that, given his ideal conditions, it would be so.

The second main point raised by critics of the General Will is whether in defining it as a will directed solely to the common interest, Rousseau means to exclude acts of public immorality and short-sightedness. He answers the questions in different ways. First, an act of public immorality would be merely an unanimous instance of selfishness, different in no particular, from similar acts less unanimous, and therefore forming no part of a General Will. Secondly, a mere ignorance of our own and the State's good, entirely unprompted by selfish desires, does not make our will anti-social or individual. "The general will is always right and tends to the public advantage; but it does not follow that the deliberations of the people are always equally correct. Our will is always for our own good, but we do not always see what that is: the people is never corrupted, but it is often deceived, and on such occasions only does it seem to will what is bad" (Book II, chap. iii). It is impossible to acquit Rousseau in some of the passages in which he treats of the General Will, of something worse than obscurity—positive contradiction. It is probable, indeed, that he never quite succeeded in getting his view clear in his own mind; there is nearly always, in his treatment of it, a certain amount of muddle and fluctuation. These difficulties the student must be left to worry out for himself; it is only possible to present, in outline, what Rousseau meant to convey.

The treatment of the General Will in the *Political Economy* is brief and lucid, and furnishes the best guide to his meaning. The definition of it in this work, which has already been quoted, is followed by a short account of the nature of *general wills* as a whole. "Every political society is composed of other smaller societies of various kinds, each of which has its interest and rules of conduct; but those societies which everybody perceives, because they have an external or authorised form, are not the only ones that actually exist in the State: all individuals who are united by a common interest compose as many others, either temporary or permanent, whose influence is none the less real because it is less apparent.... The influence of all these tacit or formal associations causes by the influence of their will as many modifications of the public will. The will of these particular societies has always two relations; for the members of the association, it is a general will; for the great society, it is a particular will; and it is often right with regard to the first object and wrong as to the second. The most general will is always the most just, and the voice of the people is, in fact, the voice of God."

The General Will, Rousseau continues in substance, is always for the common good; but it is sometimes divided into smaller general wills, which are wrong in relation to it. The supremacy of the great General Will is "the first principle of public economy and the fundamental rule of government." In this passage, which differs only in clearness and simplicity from others in the *Social Contract* itself, it is easy to see how far Rousseau had in his mind a perfectly definite idea. Every association of several persons creates a new common will; every association of a permanent character has already a "personality" of its own, and in consequence a "general" will; the State, the highest known form of association, is a fully developed moral and collective being with a common will which is, in the highest sense yet known to us, general. All such wills are general only for the members of the associations Which exercise them; for outsiders, or rather for other associations, they are purely particular wills. This applies even to the State; "for, in relation to what is outside it, the State becomes a simple being, an individual" (*Social Contract*, Book I, chap. vii). In certain passages in the *Social Contract*, in his criticism of the Abbé de Saint-Pierre's *Project of Perpetual Peace*, and in the second chapter of the original draft of the *Social Contract*, Rousseau takes into account the possibility of a still higher individual, "the federation of the world." In the *Political Economy*, thinking of the nation-state, he affirms what in the *Social Contract* (Book II, chap. iii) he denies of the city, and recognises that the life of a nation is made up of the whole complex of its institutions, and that the existence of lesser general wills is not necessarily a menace to the General Will of the State. In the *Social Contract*, he only treats of these lesser wills in relation to the government, which, he shows, has a will of its own, general for its members, but particular for the State as a whole (Book III, chap. ii). This governmental will he there prefers to call *corporate will*, and by this name it will be convenient to distinguish the lesser general wills from the General Will of the State that is over them all.

So far, there is no great difficulty; but in discussing the infallibility of the General Will we are on more dangerous ground. Rousseau's treatment here clearly oscillates between regarding it as a purely ideal conception, to which human institutions can only approximate, and holding it to be realised actually in every republican State, *i.e.* wherever the people is the Sovereign in fact as well as in right. Book IV, chap. ii is the most startling passage expressing the latter view. "When in the popular assembly a law is proposed, what the people is asked is not exactly whether it accepts or rejects the proposal, but whether it is in conformity with the general will, which is its will.... When, therefore, the opinion that is contrary to my own prevails, this proves neither more nor less than that I was mistaken, and that what I thought to be the general will was not so."

On his own principles laid down elsewhere, Rousseau would have to admit that it proves nothing of the sort, except in so far as the other voters have been guided by the general interest. Though he sometimes affirms the opposite, there is no security on his principles that the will of the majority will be the General Will. At the most it can only be said that there is a greater chance of its being general than of the will of any selected class of persons not being led away by corporate interests. The justification of democracy is not that it is always right, even in intention, but that it is more general than any other kind of supreme power.

Fundamentally, however, the doctrine of the General Will is independent of these contradictions. Apart from Kant's narrow and rigid logic, it is essentially one with his doctrine of the autonomy of the will. Kant takes Rousseau's political theory, and applies it to ethics as a whole. The germ of mis application is already found in Rousseau's own work; for he protests more than once against attempts to treat moral and political philosophy apart, as distinct studies, and asserts their absolute unity. This is brought out clearly in the *Social Contract* (Book I, chap. viii), where he is speaking of the change brought about by the establishment of society. "The passage from the state of nature to the civil state produces a very remarkable change in man, by substituting justice for instinct in his conduct, and giving his actions the morality they had hitherto lacked.... What man loses by the social contract is his natural liberty and an unlimited right to everything he tries to get and succeeds in getting; what he gains is civil liberty ... which is limited by the general will.... We might, over and above all this, add to what man acquires in the civil state *moral liberty, which alone makes him truly master of himself; for the mere impulse of appetite is slavery, while obedience to a law which we prescribe to ourselves is liberty.*"

This one chapter contains the gist of the Kantian moral philosophy, and makes it quite clear that Rousseau perceived its application to ethics as well as to politics. The morality of our acts consists in their being directed in accordance with universal law; acts in which we are guided merely by our passions are not moral. Further, man can only possess freedom when his whole being is unified in the pursuit of a single end; and, as his whole being can be unified only in pursuit of a rational end, which alone excludes contradiction, only moral acts, only men directing their lives by universal law, are free. In Kantian language, the will is autonomous (*i.e.* prescribes to itself its own law) only when it is directed to a universal end; when it is guided by selfish passions, or particular considerations, it is heteronomous (*i.e.* receives its law from something external to itself), and in bondage. Rousseau, as he says (Book I, chap. viii), was not directly concerned with the ethical sense of the word "liberty," and Kant was, therefore, left to develop the doctrine into a system; but the phrases of this chapter prove false the view that the doctrine of a Real Will arises first in connection with politics, and is only transferred thence to moral philosophy. Rousseau bases his political doctrine throughout on his view of human freedom; it is because man is a free agent capable of being determined by a universal law prescribed by himself that the State is in like manner capable of realising the General Will, that is, of prescribing to itself and its members a similar universal law.

The General Will, then, is the application of human freedom to political institutions. Before the value of this conception can be determined, there is a criticism to be met. The freedom which is realised in the General Will, we are told, is the freedom of the State *as a whole*; but the State exists to secure *individual* freedom for its members. A free State may be tyrannical; a despot may allow his subjects every freedom. What guarantee is there that the State, in freeing itself, will not enslave its members? This criticism has been made with such regularity that it has to be answered in some detail.

"The problem is to find a form of association which will defend and protect with the whole common force the person and goods of each associate, and in which each, while uniting himself with all, may still obey himself alone, and remain as free as before." "The clauses of the contract ... are everywhere the same and everywhere tacitly admitted and recognised.... These clauses, properly understood, may be reduced to one—the total alienation of each associate, together with all his rights, to the whole community...; for, if the individuals retained certain rights, as there would be no common superior to decide between them and the public, each, being on one point his own judge, would ask to be so on all, and the state of nature would continue" (Book I, chap. vi). Rousseau sees clearly that it is impossible to place any limits upon the power of the State; when the people combine into a State, they must in the end submit to be guided in all things by the will of the effective majority. Limited Sovereignty is a contradiction in terms; the Sovereign has a right to all that reason allows it, and as soon as reason demands that the State shall interfere, no appeal to individual rights can be made. What is best for the State must be suffered by the individual. This, however, is very far from meaning that the ruling power ought, or has the moral right, to interfere in every particular case. Rousseau has been subjected to much foolish criticism because, after upholding the State's absolute supremacy, he goes on (Book II, chap. iv) to speak of "the limits of the sovereign power." There is no contradiction whatsoever. Wherever State intervention is for the best, the State has a right to intervene; but it has no moral right, though it must have a legal right, to intervene where it is not for the best. The General Will, being always in the right, will intervene only when intervention is proper. "The Sovereign," therefore, "cannot impose upon its subjects any fetters that are useless to the community, nor can it even wish to do so." As, however, the infallibility of the General Will is not enough to make the State infallible, there still remains an objection. Since the General Will cannot always be arrived at, who is to judge whether an act of intervention is justified? Rousseau's answer fails to satisfy many of his critics. "Each man alienates, I admit, by the social compact, only such part of his powers, goods and liberty as it is important for the community to control; but it must also be granted that the Sovereign is sole judge of what is important." This, we are told, is mere State tyranny over again. But how is it possible to avoid such a conclusion? Rousseau has already given his reasons for objecting to a limited Sovereignty (Book I, chap. vi): it follows absolutely that we must take the best machinery we can find for the execution of the State's functions. No doubt the machinery will be imperfect; but we can only try to get as near the General Will as possible, without hoping to realise it fully.

The answer, therefore, to the critics who hold that, in securing civil liberty Rousseau has sacrificed the individual may be put after this fashion. Liberty is not a merely negative conception; it does not consist solely in the absence of restraint. The purest individualist, Herbert Spencer for example, would grant that a certain amount of State interference is necessary to *secure* liberty; but as soon as this idea of securing liberty is admitted in the smallest degree, the whole idea has undergone profound modification. It can no longer be claimed that every interference on the part of the State lessens the liberty of the individual; the "liberty-fund" theory is as untenable as that of the "wages-fund": the members of a State may be more free when all are restrained from doing one another mutual damage than when any one is left "free" to enslave another or be himself enslaved. This principle once admitted, the precise amount of State interference that is necessary to secure freedom will be always a matter for particular discussion; every case must be decided on its own merits, and, in right, the Sovereign will be omnipotent, or subject only to the law of reason.

It has often been held that Rousseau cannot really have inspired the French Revolution because this view is totally inconsistent with the "rights of man," which the revolutionaries so fervently proclaimed. If every right is alienated in the Social Contract, what sense can there be in talking of "natural rights" afterwards? This, however, is to misrepresent Rousseau's position. The rights of man as they are preached by the modern individualist, are not the rights of which Rousseau and the revolutionaries were thinking.

We have seen that the theory of the *Social Contract* is founded on human freedom: this freedom carries with it, in Rousseau's view, the guarantee of its own permanence; it is inalienable and indestructible. When, therefore, government becomes despotic, it has no more right over its subjects than the master has over his slave (Book I, chap. iv); the question is then purely one of might. In such cases, appeal may be made either to the terms of the Social Contract, or, putting the same idea another way, to the "natural right" of human freedom. This natural right is in no sense inconsistent with the complete alienation supposed in the Contract; for the Contract itself reposes on it and guarantees its maintenance. The Sovereign must, therefore, treat all its members alike; but, so long as it does this, it remains omnipotent. If it leaves the general for the particular, and treats one man better than another, it ceases to be Sovereign; but equality is already presupposed in the terms of the Contract.

It is more profitable to attack Rousseau for his facile identification of the interests of each of the citizens with those of all; but here, too, most of the critics have abused their opportunity. He does not maintain that there can be no opposition between a man's particular interests and the General Will as present in him; on the contrary, he explicitly and consistently affirms the presence of such opposition (Book I, chap. vii). What he asserts is, first, that the Sovereign, as such, cannot have any interest contrary to the interest of the citizens as a whole—that is obvious; and, secondly, that it cannot have an interest contrary to that of any individual. The second point Rousseau proves by showing that the omnipotence of the Sovereign is essential to the preservation of society, which in turn is necessary for the individual. His argument, however, really rests on the fundamental character of the General Will. He would admit that, in any actual State, the apparent interest of the many might often conflict with that of the few; but he would contend that the *real* interest of State and individual alike, being subject to universal law could not be such as to conflict with any other *real* interest. The interest of the State, in so far as it is directed by the General Will, must be the interest of every individual, in so far as he is guided by his *real* will, that is, in so far as he is acting universally, rationally and autonomously.

Thus the justification of Rousseau's theory of liberty returns to the point from which it set out—the omnipotence of the *real will* in State and individual. It is in this sense that he speaks of man in the State as "forced to be free" by the General Will, much as Kant might speak of a man's lower nature as forced to be free by the universal mandate of his higher, more real and more rational will. It is in this recognition of the State as a moral being, with powers of determination similar to the powers of the individual mind, that the significance of the General Will ultimately lies. Even, however, among those who have recognised its meaning, there are some who deny its value as a conception of political philosophy. If, they say, the General Will is not the Will of All, if it cannot be arrived at by a majority vote or by any system of voting whatsoever, then it is nothing; it is a mere abstraction, neither general, nor a I will. This is, of course, precisely the criticism to which Kant's "real will" is often subjected. Clearly, it must be granted at once that the General Will does not form the whole actual content of the will of every citizen. Regarded as actual, it must always be qualified by "in so far as" or its equivalent. This, however, is so far from destroying the value of the conception that therein lies its whole value. In seeking the universal basis of society, we are not seeking anything that is wholly actualised in any State, though we must be seeking something which exists, more or less perfectly, in every State.

The point of the Social Contract theory, as Rousseau states it, is that legitimate society exists by the consent of the people, and acts by popular will. Active will, and not force or even mere consent, is the basis of the "republican" State, which can only possess this character because individual wills are not really self-sufficient and separate, but complementary and inter-dependent. The answer to the question "Why ought I to obey the General Will?" is that the General Will exists in me and not outside me. I am "obeying only myself," as Rousseau says. The State is not a mere accident of human history, a mere device for the protection of life and property; it responds to a fundamental need of human nature, and is rooted in the character of the individuals who compose it. The whole complex of human institutions is not a mere artificial structure; it is the expression of the mutual dependence and fellowship of men. If it means anything, the theory of the General Will means that the State is natural, and the "state of nature" an abstraction. Without this basis of will and natural need, no society could for a moment subsist; the State exists and claims our obedience because it is a natural extension of our personality.

The problem, however, still remains of making the General Will, in any particular State, active and conscious. It is clear that there are States in which visible and recognised institutions hardly answer in any respect to its requirements. Even in such States, however, there is a limit to tyranny; deep down, in immemorial customs with which the despot dare not interfere, the General Will is still active and important. It does not reside merely in the outward and visible organisation of social institutions, in that complex of formal associations which we may call the State; its roots go deeper and its branches spread further. It is realised, in greater or less degree, in the whole life of the community, in the entire complex of private and public relations which, in the widest sense, may be called Society. We may recognise it not only in a Parliament, a Church, a University or a Trade Union, but also in the most intimate human relationships, and the most trivial, as well as the most vital, social customs.

But, if all these things go to the making of the General Will in every community, the General Will has, for politics, primarily a narrower sense. The problem here is to secure its supremacy in the official institutions and public councils of the nation. This is the question to which Rousseau chiefly addressed himself. Here, too, we shall find the General Will the best possible conception for the guidance of political endeavour For the General Will is realised not when that is done which is best for the community, but when, in addition, the community as a whole has willed the doing of it. The General Will demands not only good government, but also self-government—not only rational conduct, but good-will. This is what some of Rousseau's admirers are apt to forget when they use his argument, as he himself was sometimes inclined to use it, in support of pure aristocracy. Rousseau said that aristocracy was the best of all governments, but he said also that it was the worst of all usurpers of Sovereignty. Nor must it be forgotten that he expressly specified elective aristocracy. *There is no General Will unless the people wills the good.* General Will may be embodied in one man willing universally; but it can only be embodied in the State when the mass of the citizens so wills. The will must be "general" in two senses: in the sense in which Rousseau used the word, it must be general in its object, *i.e.* universal; but it must also be generally held, *i.e.* common to all or to the majority.[1]

The General Will is, then, above all a universal and, in the Kantian sense, a "rational" will. It would be possible to find in Rousseau many more anticipations of the views of Kant; but it is better here to confine comment to an important difference between them. It is surprising to find in Kant, the originator of modern "intellectualism," and in Rousseau, the great apostle of "sentiment," an essentially similar view on the nature and function of the will. Their views, however, present a difference; for, whereas the moving force of Kant's moral imperative is purely "rational," Rousseau finds the sanction of his General Will in human feeling itself. As we can see from a passage in the

---

[1] The term "general" will means, in Rousseau, not so much "will held by several persons," as will having a general (universal) object. This is often misunderstood; but the mistake matters the less, because the General Will must, in fact, be both.

original draft of the *Social Contract,* the General Will remains purely rational. "No-one will dispute that the General Will is in each individual a pure act of the understanding, which reasons while the passions are silent on what a man may demand of his neighbour and on what his neighbour has a right to demand of him." The will remains purely rational, but Rousseau feels that it needs an external motive power. "If natural law," he writes, "were written only on the tablets of human reason it would be incapable of guiding the greater part of our actions; but it is also graven on the heart of man in characters that cannot be effaced, and it is there it speaks to him more strongly than all the precepts of the philosophers" (from an unfinished essay on *The State of War*). The nature of this guiding sentiment is explained in the *Discourse on Inequality* (p. 197, note 2), where egoism (*amour-propre*) is contrasted with self-respect (*amour de soi*). Naturally, Rousseau holds, man does not want everything for himself, and nothing for others. "Egoism" and "altruism" are both one-sided qualities arising out of the perversion of man's, "natural goodness." "Man is born good," that is, man's nature really makes him desire only to be treated as one among others, to share equally. This natural love of equality (*amour de soi*) includes love of others as well as love of self, and egoism, loving one's self at the expense of others, is an unnatural and perverted condition. The "rational" precepts of the General Will, therefore, find an echo in the heart of the "natural" man, and, if we can only secure the human being against perversion by existing societies, the General Will can be made actual.

This is the meeting-point of Rousseau's educational with his political theory. His view as a whole can be studied only by taking together the *Social Contract* and the *Emile* as explained by the *Letters on the Mount* and other works. The fundamental dogma of the natural goodness of man finds no place directly in the *Social Contract*; but it lurks behind the whole of his political theory, and is indeed, throughout, his master-conception. His educational, his religious, his political and his ethical ideas are all inspired by a single consistent attitude. Here we have been attending only to his political theory; in the volume which is to follow, containing the *Letters on the Mount* and other works, some attempt will be made to draw the various threads together and estimate his work as a whole. The political works, however, can be read separately, and the *Social Contract* itself is still by far the best of all text-books of political philosophy. Rousseau's political influence, so far from being dead, is every day increasing; and as new generations and new classes of men come to the study of his work, his conceptions, often hazy and undeveloped, but nearly always of lasting value, will assuredly form the basis of a new political philosophy, in which they will be taken up and transformed. This new philosophy is the work of the future; but, rooted upon the conception of Rousseau, it will stretch far back into the past. Of our time, it will be for all time; its solutions will be at once relatively permanent and ceaselessly progressive.

G. D. H. COLE.

BOOK I

I mean to inquire if, in the civil order, there can be any sure and legitimate rule of administration, men being taken as they are and laws as they might be. In this inquiry I shall endeavour always to unite what right sanctions with what is prescribed by interest, in order that justice and utility may in no case be divided.

I enter upon my task without proving the importance of the subject I shall be asked if I am a prince or a legislator, to write on politics. I answer that I am neither, and that is why I do so. If I were a prince or a legislator, I should not waste time in saying what wants doing; I should do it, or hold my peace.

As I was born a citizen of a free State, and a member of the Sovereign, I feel that, however feeble the influence my voice can have on public affairs, the right of voting on them makes it my duty to study them: and I am happy, when I reflect upon governments, to find my inquiries always furnish me with new reasons for loving that of my own country.

CHAPTER I: SUBJECT OF THE FIRST BOOK

Man is born free; and everywhere he is in chains. One thinks himself the master of others, and still remains a greater slave than they. How did this change come about? I do not know. What can make it legitimate? That question I think I can answer.

If I took into account only force, and the effects derived from it, I should say: "As long as a people is compelled to obey, and obeys, it does well; as soon as it can shake off the yoke, and shakes it off, it does still better; for, regaining its liberty by the same right as took it away, either it is justified in resuming it, or there was no justification for those who took it away." But the social order is a sacred right which is the basis of all other rights. Nevertheless, this right does not come from nature, and must therefore be founded on conventions. Before coming to that, I have to prove what I have just asserted.

CHAPTER II: THE FIRST SOCIETIES

The most ancient of all societies, and the only one that is natural is the family: and even so the children remain attached to the father only so long as they need him for their preservation. As soon as this need ceases, the natural bond is dissolved. The children, released from the obedience they owed to the father, and the father, released from the care he owed his children, return equally to independence. If they remain united, they continue so no longer naturally, but voluntarily; and the family itself is then maintained only by convention.

This common liberty results from the nature of man. His first law is to provide for his own preservation, his first cares are those which he owes to himself; and, as soon as he reaches years of discretion, he is the sole judge of the proper means of preserving himself, and consequently becomes his own master.

The family then may be called the first model of political societies: the ruler corresponds to the father, and the people to the children; and all, being born free and equal, alienate their liberty only for their own advantage. The whole difference is that, in the family, the love of the father for his children repays him for the care he takes of them, while, in the State, the pleasure of commanding takes the place of the love which the chief cannot have for the peoples under him.

Grotius denies that all human power is established in favour of the governed, and quotes slavery as an example. His usual method of reasoning is constantly to establish right by fact.[1] It would be possible to employ a more logical method, but none could be more favourable to tyrants.

It is then, according to Grotius, doubtful whether the human race belongs to a hundred men, or that hundred men to the human race: and, throughout his book, he seems to incline to the former alternative, which is also the view of Hobbes. On this showing, the human species is divided into so many herds of cattle, each with its ruler, who keeps guard over them for the purpose of devouring them.

As a shepherd is of a nature superior to that of his flock, the shepherds of men, *i.e.* their rulers, are of a nature superior to that of the peoples under them. Thus, Philo tells us, the Emperor Caligula reasoned, concluding equally well either that kings were gods, or that men were beasts.

The reasoning of Caligula agrees with that of Hobbes and Grotius. Aristotle, before any of them, had said that men are by no means equal naturally, but that some are born for slavery, and others for dominion.

Aristotle was right; but he took the effect for the cause. Nothing can be more certain than that every man born in slavery is born for slavery. Slaves lose everything in their chains, even the desire of escaping from them: they love their servitude, as the comrades of Ulysses loved their brutish condition.[2] If then there are slaves by nature, it is because there have been slaves against nature. Force made the first slaves, and their cowardice perpetuated the condition.

I have said nothing of King Adam, or Emperor Noah, father of the three great monarchs who shared out the universe, like the children of Saturn, whom some scholars have recognised in them. I trust to getting due thanks for my moderation; for, being a direct descendant of one of these princes, perhaps of the eldest branch, how do I know that a verification of titles might not leave me the legitimate king of the human race? In any case, there can be no doubt that Adam was sovereign of the world, as Robinson Crusoe was of his island, as long as he was its only inhabitant; and this empire had the advantage that the monarch, safe on his throne, had no rebellions, wars, or conspirators to fear.

CHAPTER III: THE RIGHT OF THE STRONGEST

The strongest is never strong enough to be always the master, unless he transforms strength into right, and obedience into duty. Hence the right of the strongest, which, though to all seeming meant ironically, is really laid down as a fundamental principle. But are we never to have an explanation of this phrase? Force is a physical power, and I fail to see what moral effect it can have. To yield to force is an act of necessity, not of will—at the most, an act of prudence. In what sense can it be a duty?

Suppose for a moment that this so-called "right" exists. I maintain that the sole result is a mass of inexplicable nonsense. For, if force creates right, the effect changes with the cause: every force that is greater than the first succeeds to its right. As soon as it is

---

[1] "Learned inquiries into public right are often only the history of past abuses; and troubling to study them too deeply is a profitless infatuation" (*Essay on the Interests of France in Relation to its Neighbours*, by the Marquis d'Argenson). This is exactly what Grotius has done.

[2] See a short treatise of Plutarch's entitled "That Animals Reason."

possible to disobey with impunity, disobedience is legitimate; and, the strongest being always in the right, the only thing that matters is to act so as to become the strongest. But what kind of right is that which perishes when force fails? If we must obey perforce, there is no need to obey because we ought; and if we are not forced to obey, we are under no obligation to do so. Clearly, the word "right" adds nothing to force: in this connection, it means absolutely nothing.

Obey the powers that be. If this means yield to force, it is a good precept, but superfluous: I can answer for its never being violated. All power comes from God, I admit; but so does all sickness: does that mean that we are forbidden to call in the doctor? A brigand surprises me at the edge of a wood: must I not merely surrender my purse on compulsion; but, even if I could withhold it, am I in conscience bound to give it up? For certainly the pistol he holds is also a power.

Let us then admit that force does not create right, and that we are obliged to obey only legitimate powers. In that case, my original question recurs.

CHAPTER IV: SLAVERY

Since no man has a natural authority over his fellow, and force creates no right, we must conclude that conventions form the basis of all legitimate authority among men.

If an individual, says Grotius, can alienate his liberty and make himself the slave of a master, why could not a whole people do the same and make itself subject to a king? There are in this passage plenty of ambiguous words which would need explaining; but let us confine ourselves to the word *alienate*. To alienate is to give or to sell. Now, a man who becomes the slave of another does not give himself; he sells himself, at the least for his subsistence: but for what does a people sell itself? A king is so far from furnishing his subjects with their subsistence that he gets his own only from them; and, according to Rabelais, kings do not live on nothing. Do subjects then give their persons on condition that the king takes their goods also? I fail to see what they have left to preserve.

It will be said that the despot assures his subjects civil tranquillity. Granted; but what do they gain, if the wars his ambition brings down upon them, his insatiable avidity, and the vexatious conduct of his ministers press harder on them than their own dissensions would have done? What do they gain, if the very tranquillity they enjoy is one of their miseries? Tranquillity is found also in dungeons; but is that enough to make them desirable places to live in? The Greeks imprisoned in the cave of the Cyclops lived there very tranquilly, while they were awaiting their turn to be devoured.

To say that a man gives himself gratuitously, is to say what is absurd and inconceivable; such an act is null and illegitimate, from the mere fact that he who does it is out of his mind. To say the same of a whole people is to suppose a people of madmen; and madness creates no right.

Even if each man could alienate himself, he could not alienate his children: they are born men and free; their liberty belongs to them, and no one but they has the right to dispose of it. Before they come to years of discretion, the father can, in their name, lay down conditions for their preservation and well-being, but he cannot give them, irrevocably and without conditions: such a gift is contrary to the ends of nature, and exceeds the rights of paternity. It would therefore be necessary, in order to legitimise an arbitrary government, that in every generation the people should be in a position to accept or reject it; but, were this so, the government would be no longer arbitrary.

To renounce liberty is to renounce being a man, to surrender the rights of humanity and even its duties. For him who renounces everything no indemnity is possible. Such a renunciation is incompatible with man's nature; to remove all liberty from his will is to remove all morality from his acts. Finally, it is an empty and contradictory convention that sets up, on the one side, absolute authority, and, on the other, unlimited obedience. Is it not clear that we can be under no obligation to a person from whom we have the right to exact everything? Does not this condition alone, in the absence of equivalence or exchange, in itself involve the nullity of the act? For what right can my slave have against me, when all that he has belongs to me, and, his right being mine, this right of mine against myself is a phrase devoid of meaning?

Grotius and the rest find in war another origin for the so-called right of slavery. The victor having, as they hold, the right of killing the vanquished, the latter can buy back his life at the price of his liberty; and this convention is the more legitimate because it is to the advantage of both parties.

But it is clear that this supposed right to kill the conquered is by no means deducible from the state of war. Men, from the mere fact that, while they are living in their primitive independence, they have no mutual relations stable enough to constitute either the state of peace or the state of war, cannot be naturally enemies. War is constituted by a relation between things, and not between persons; and, as the state of war cannot arise out of simple personal relations, but only out of real relations, private war, or war of man with man, can exist neither in the state of nature, where there is no constant property, nor in the social state, where everything is under the authority of the laws.

Individual combats, duels and encounters, are acts which cannot constitute a state; while the private wars, authorised by the Establishments of Louis IX, King of France, and suspended by the Peace of God, are abuses of feudalism, in itself an absurd system if ever there was one, and contrary to the principles of natural right and to all good polity.

War then is a relation, not between man and man, but between State and State, and individuals are enemies only accidentally, not as men, nor even as citizens,[3] but as soldiers; not as members of their country, but as its defenders. Finally, each State can have for enemies only other States, and not men; for between things disparate in nature there can be no real relation.

Furthermore, this principle is in conformity with the established rules of all times and the constant practice of all civilised peoples. Declarations of war are intimations less to powers than to their subjects. The foreigner, whether king, individual, or people, who robs, kills or detains the subjects, without declaring war on the prince, is not an enemy, but a brigand. Even in real war, a just prince, while laying hands, in the enemy's country, on all that belongs to the public, respects the lives and goods of individuals: he respects rights on which his own are founded. The object of the war being the destruction of the hostile State, the other side has a right to kill its defenders, while they are bearing arms; but as soon as they lay them down and surrender, they cease to be enemies or instruments of the enemy, and become once more merely men, whose life no one has any right to take. Sometimes it is possible to kill the State without killing a single one of its members;

---

[3] The Romans, who understood and respected the right of war more than any other nation on earth, carried their scruples on this head so far that a citizen was not allowed to serve as a volunteer without engaging himself expressly against the enemy, and against such and such an enemy by name. A legion in which the younger Cato was seeing his first service under Popilius having been reconstructed, the elder Cato wrote to Popilius that, if he wished his son to continue serving under him, he must administer to him a new military oath, because, the first having been annulled, he was no longer able to bear arms against the enemy. The same Cato wrote to his son telling him to take great care not to go into battle before taking this new oath. I know that the siege of Clusium and other isolated events can be quoted against me; but I am citing laws and customs. The Romans are the people that least often transgressed its laws; and no other people has had such good ones.

and war gives no right which is not necessary to the gaining of its object. These principles are not those of Grotius: they are not based on the authority of poets, but derived from the nature of reality and based on reason.

The right of conquest has no foundation other than the right of the strongest. If war does not give the conqueror the right to massacre the conquered peoples, the right to enslave them cannot be based upon a right which does not exist No one has a right to kill an enemy except when he cannot make him a slave, and the right to enslave him cannot therefore be derived from the right to kill him. It is accordingly an unfair exchange to make him buy at the price of his liberty his life, over which the victor holds no right. Is it not clear that there is a vicious circle in founding the right of life and death on the right of slavery, and the right of slavery on the right of life and death?

Even if we assume this terrible right to kill everybody, I maintain that a slave made in war, or a conquered people, is under no obligation to a master, except to obey him as far as he is compelled to do so. By taking an equivalent for his life, the victor has not done him a favour; instead of killing him without profit, he has killed him usefully. So far then is he from acquiring over him any authority in addition to that of force, that the state of war continues to subsist between them: their mutual relation is the effect of it, and the usage of the right of war does not imply a treaty of peace. A convention has indeed been made; but this convention, so far from destroying the state of war, presupposes its continuance.

So, from whatever aspect we regard the question, the right of slavery is null and void, not only as being illegitimate, but also because it is absurd and meaningless. The words *slave* and *right* contradict each other, and are mutually exclusive. It will always be equally foolish for a man to say to a man or to a people: "I make with you a convention wholly at your expense and wholly to my advantage; I shall keep it as long as I like, and you will keep it as long as I like."

CHAPTER V: THAT WE MUST ALWAYS GO BACK TO A FIRST CONVENTION

Even if I granted all that I have been refuting, the friends of despotism would be no better off. There will always be a great difference between subduing a multitude and ruling a society. Even if scattered individuals were successively enslaved by one man, however numerous they might be, I still see no more than a master and his slaves, and certainly not a people and its ruler; I see what may be termed an aggregation, but not an association; there is as yet neither public good nor body politic. The man in question, even if he has enslaved half the world, is still only an individual; his interest, apart from that of others, is still a purely private interest. If this same man comes to die, his empire, after him, remains scattered and without unity, as an oak falls and dissolves into a heap of ashes when the fire has consumed it.

A people, says Grotius, can give itself to a king. Then, according to Grotius, a people is a people before it gives itself. The gift is itself a civil act, and implies public deliberation. It would be better, before examining the act by which a people gives itself to a king, to examine that by which it has become a people; for this act, being necessarily prior to the other, is the true foundation of society.

Indeed, if there were no prior convention, where, unless the election were unanimous, would be the obligation on the minority to submit to the choice of the majority? How have a hundred men who wish for a master the right to vote on behalf of ten who do not? The law of majority voting is itself something established by convention, and presupposes unanimity, on one occasion at least.

CHAPTER VI: THE SOCIAL COMPACT

I suppose men to have reached the point at which the obstacles in the way of their preservation in the state of nature show their power of resistance to be greater than the resources at the disposal of each individual for his maintenance in that state. That primitive condition can then subsist no longer; and the human race would perish unless it changed its manner of existence.

But, as men cannot engender new forces, but only unite and direct existing ones, they have no other means of preserving themselves than the formation, by aggregation, of a sum of forces great enough to overcome the resistance. These they have to bring into play by means of a single motive power, and cause to act in concert.

This sum of forces can arise only where several persons come together: but, as the force and liberty of each man are the chief instruments of his self-preservation, how can he pledge them without harming his own interests, and neglecting the care he owes to himself? This difficulty, in its bearing on my present subject, may be stated in the following terms—

"The problem is to find a form of association which will defend and protect with the whole common force the person and goods of each associate, and in which each, while uniting himself with all, may still obey himself alone, and remain as free as before." This is the fundamental problem of which the *Social Contract* provides the solution.

The clauses of this contract are so determined by the nature of the act that the slightest modification would make them vain and ineffective; so that, although they have perhaps never been formally set forth, they are everywhere the same and everywhere tacitly admitted and recognised, until, on the violation of the social compact, each regains his original rights and resumes his natural liberty, while losing the conventional liberty in favour of which he renounced it.

These clauses, properly understood, may be reduced to one—the total alienation of each associate, together with all his rights, to the whole community for, in the first place, as each gives himself absolutely, the conditions are the same for all; and, this being so, no one has any interest in making them burdensome to others.

Moreover, the alienation being without reserve, the union is as perfect as it can be, and no associate has anything more to demand: for, if the individuals retained certain rights, as there would be no common superior to decide between them and the public, each, being on one point his own judge, would ask to be so on all; the state of nature would thus continue, and the association would necessarily become inoperative or tyrannical.

Finally, each man, in giving himself to all, gives himself to nobody; and as there is no associate over whom he does not acquire the same right as he yields others over himself, he gains an equivalent for everything he loses, and an increase of force for the preservation of what he has.

If then we discard from the social compact what is not of its essence, we shall find that it reduces itself to the following terms—

"Each of us puts his person and all his power in common under the supreme direction of the general will, and, in our corporate capacity, we receive each member as an indivisible part of the whole."

At once, in place of the individual personality of each contracting party, this act of association creates a moral and collective body, composed of as many members as the assembly contains votes, and receiving from this act its unity, its common identity, its life and its will. This public person, so formed by the union of all other persons, formerly took the name of *city*,[4] and now takes that of *Republic* or *body politic*; it is called by its members *State* when passive, *Sovereign* when active, and *Power* when compared with others like itself. Those who are associated in it take collectively the name of *people*, and severally are called *citizens*, as sharing in the sovereign power, and *subjects*, as being under the laws of the State. But these terms are often confused and taken one for another: it is enough to know how to distinguish them when they are being used with precision.

CHAPTER VII: THE SOVEREIGN

This formula shows us that the act of association comprises a mutual undertaking between the public and the individuals, and that each individual, in making a contract, as we may say, with himself, is bound in a double capacity; as a member of the Sovereign he is bound to the individuals, and as a member of the State to the Sovereign. But the maxim of civil right, that no one is bound by undertakings made to himself, does not apply in this case; for there is a great difference between incurring an obligation to yourself and incurring one to a whole of which you form a part.

Attention must further be called to the fact that public deliberation, while competent to bind all the subjects to the Sovereign, because of the two different capacities in which each of them may be regarded, cannot, for the opposite reason, bind the Sovereign to itself; and that it is consequently against the nature of the body politic for the Sovereign to impose on itself a law which it cannot infringe. Being able to regard itself in only one capacity, it is in the position of an individual who makes a contract with himself; and this makes it clear that there neither is nor can be any kind of fundamental law binding on the body of the people—not even the social contract itself. This does not mean that the body politic cannot enter into undertakings with others, provided the contract is not infringed by them; for in relation to what is external to it, it becomes a simple being, an individual.

But the body politic or the Sovereign, drawing its being wholly from the sanctity of the contract, can never bind itself, even to an outsider, to do anything derogatory to the original act, for instance, to alienate any part of itself, or to submit to another Sovereign. Violation of the act by which it exists would be self-annihilation; and that which is itself nothing can create nothing.

As soon as this multitude is so united in one body, it is impossible to offend against one of the members without attacking the body, and still more to offend against the body without the members resenting it. Duty and interest therefore equally oblige the two contracting parties to give each other help; and the same men should seek to combine, in their double capacity, all the advantages dependent upon that capacity.

---

[4] The real meaning of this word has been almost wholly lost in modern times; most people mistake a town for a city, and a townsman for a citizen. They do not know that houses make a town, but citizens a city. The same mistake long ago cost the Carthaginians dear. I have never read of the title of citizens being given to the subjects of any prince, not even the ancient Macedonians or the English of to-day, though they are nearer liberty than any one else. The French alone everywhere familiarly adopt the name of citizens, because, as can be seen from their dictionaries, they have no idea of its meaning; otherwise they would be guilty in usurping it, of the crime of *lèse-majesté*: among them, the name expresses a virtue, and not a right. When Bodin spoke of our citizens and townsmen, he fell into a bad blunder in taking the one class for the other. M. d'Alembert has avoided the error, and, in his article on Geneva, has clearly distinguished the four orders of men (or even five, counting mere foreigners) who dwell in our town, of which two only compose the Republic. No other French writer, to my knowledge, has understood the real meaning of the word citizen.

Again, the Sovereign, being formed wholly of the individuals who compose it, neither has nor can have any interest contrary to theirs; and consequently the sovereign power need give no guarantee to its subjects, because it is impossible for the body to wish to hurt all its members. We shall also see later on that It cannot hurt any in particular. The Sovereign, merely by virtue of what it is, is always what it should be.

This, however, is not the case with the relation of the subjects to the Sovereign, which, despite the common interest, would have no security that they would fulfil their undertakings, unless it found means to assure itself of their fidelity.

In fact, each individual, as a man, may have a particular will contrary or dissimilar to the general will which he has as a citizen. His particular interest may speak to him quite differently from the common interest: his absolute and naturally independent existence may make him look upon what he owes to the common cause as a gratuitous contribution, the loss of which will do less harm to others than the payment of it is burdensome to himself; and, regarding the moral person which constitutes the State as a persona ficta, because not a man, he may wish to enjoy the rights of citizenship without being ready to fulfil the duties of a subject. The continuance of such an injustice could not but prove the undoing of the body politic.

In order then that the social compact may not be an empty formula, it tacitly includes the undertaking, which alone can give force to the rest, that whoever refuses to obey the general will shall be compelled to do so by the whole body. This means nothing less than that he will be forced to be free; for this is the condition which, by giving each citizen to his country, secures him against all personal dependence. In this lies the key to the working of the political machine; this alone legitimizes civil undertakings, which, without it, would be absurd, tyrannical, and liable to the most frightful abuses.

CHAPTER VIII: THE CIVIL STATE

The passage from the state of nature to the civil state produces a very remarkable change in man, by substituting justice, for instinct in his conduct, and giving his actions the morality they had formerly lacked. Then only, when the voice of duty takes the place of physical impulses and right of appetite, does *man*, who so far had considered only himself, find that he is forced to act on different principles, and to consult his reason before listening to his inclinations. Although, in this state, he deprives himself of some advantages which he got from nature, he gains in return others so great, his faculties are so stimulated and developed, his ideas so extended, his feelings so ennobled, and his whole soul so uplifted, that, did not the abuses of this new condition often degrade him below that which he left, he would be bound to bless continually the happy moment which took him from it for ever, and, instead of a stupid and unimaginative animal, made him an intelligent being and a man.

Let us draw up the whole account in terms easily commensurable. What man loses by the social contract in his natural liberty and an unlimited right to everything he tries to get and succeeds in getting; what he gains is civil liberty and the proprietorship of all he possesses. If we are to avoid mistake in weighing one against the other, we must clearly distinguish natural liberty, which is bounded only by the strength of the individual, from civil liberty, which is limited by the general will; and possession, which is merely the effect of force or the right of the first occupier, from property, which can be founded only on a positive title.

We might, over and above all this, add, to what man acquires in the civil state, moral liberty, which alone makes him truly master of himself; for the mere impulse of appetite is slavery, while obedience to a law which we prescribe to ourselves is liberty. But I have already said too much on this head, and the philosophical meaning of the word liberty does not now concern us.

CHAPTER IX: REAL PROPERTY

Each member of the community gives himself to it, at the moment of its foundation, just as he is, with all the resources at his command, including the goods he possesses. This act does not make possession, in changing hands, change its nature, and becomes property in the hands of the Sovereign; but, as the forces of the city are incomparably greater than those of an individual, public possession is also, in fact, stronger and more irrevocable, without being any more legitimate, at any rate from the point of view of foreigners. For the State, in relation to its members, is master of all their goods by the social contract, which, within the State, is the basis of all rights; but, in relation to other powers, it is so only by the right of the first occupier, which it holds from its members.

The right of the first occupier, though more real than the right of the strongest, becomes a real right only when the right of property has already been established. Every man has naturally a right to everything he needs; but the positive act which makes him proprietor of one thing excludes him from everything else. Having his share, he ought to keep to it, and can have no further right against the community. This is why the right of the first occupier, which in the state of nature is so weak, claims the respect of every man in civil society. In this right we are respecting not so much what belongs to another as what does not belong to ourselves.

In general, to establish the right of the first occupier over a plot of ground, the following conditions are necessary: first, the land must not yet be inhabited; secondly, a man must occupy only the amount he needs for his subsistence; and, in the third place, possession must be taken, not by an empty ceremony, but by labour and cultivation, the only sign of proprietorship that should be respected by others, in default of a legal title.

In granting the right of first occupancy to necessity and labour, are we not really stretching it as far as it can go? Is it possible to leave such a right unlimited? Is it to be enough to set foot on a plot of common ground, in order to be able to call yourself at once the master of it? Is it to be enough that a man has the strength to expel others for a moment, in order to establish his right to prevent them from ever returning? How can a man or a people seize an immense territory and keep it from the rest of the world except by a punishable usurpation, since all others are being robbed, by such an act, of the place of habitation and the means of subsistence which nature gave them in common? When Nuñez Balboa, standing on the sea-shore, took possession of the South Seas and the whole of South America in the name of the crown of Castille, was that enough to dispossess all their actual inhabitants, and to shut out from them all the princes of the world? On such a showing, these ceremonies are idly multiplied, and the Catholic King need only take possession all at once, from his apartment, of the whole universe, merely making a subsequent reservation about what was already in the possession of other princes.

We can imagine how the lands of individuals, where they were contiguous and came to be united, became the public territory, and how the right of Sovereignty, extending from the subjects over the lands they held, became at once real and personal. The possessors were thus made more dependent, and the forces at their command used to guarantee their fidelity. The advantage of this does not seem to have been felt by ancient monarchs, who called themselves King of the Persians, Scythians, or Macedonians, and seemed to regard themselves more as rulers of men than as masters of a country. Those of the present day more cleverly call themselves Kings of France, Spain, England, etc.: thus holding the land, they are quite confident of holding the inhabitants.

The peculiar fact about this alienation is that, in taking over the goods of individuals, the community, so far from despoiling them, only assures them legitimate possession, and changes usurpation into a true right and enjoyment into proprietorship. Thus the possessors, being regarded as depositaries of the public good, and having their rights, respected by all the members of the State and maintained against foreign aggression by all its forces, have, by a cession which benefits both the public and still more themselves, acquired, so to speak, all that they gave up. This paradox may easily be explained by the distinction between the rights which the Sovereign and the proprietor have over the same estate, as we shall see later on. It may also happen that men begin to unite one with another before they possess anything, and that, subsequently occupying a tract of country which is enough for all, they enjoy it in common, or share it out among themselves, either equally or according to a scale fixed by their Sovereign. However the acquisition be made, the right which each individual has to his own estate is always subordinate to the right which the community has over all: without this, there would be neither stability in the social tie, nor real force in the exercise of Sovereignty.

I shall end this chapter and this book by remarking on a fact on which the whole social system should rest: *i.e.* that, instead of destroying natural inequality, the fundamental compact substitutes, for such physical inequality as nature may have set up between men, an equality that is moral and legitimate, and that men, who may be unequal in strength or intelligence, become every one equal by convention and legal right.[5]

---

[5] Under bad governments, this equality is only apparent and illusory: it serves only to keep the pauper in his poverty and the rich man in the position he has usurped. In fact, laws are always of use to those who possess and harmful to those who have nothing: from which it follows that the social state is advantageous to men only when all have something and none too much.

BOOK II

CHAPTER I: THAT SOVEREIGNTY IS INALIENABLE

The first and most important deduction from the principles we have so far laid down is that the general will alone can direct the State according to the object for which it was instituted, *i.e.* the common good: for if the clashing of particular interests made the establishment of societies necessary, the agreement of these very interests made it possible. The common element in these different interests is what forms the social tie; and, were there no point of agreement between them all, no society could exist. It is solely on the basis of this common interest that every society should be governed.

I hold then that Sovereignty, being nothing less than the exercise of the general will, can never be alienated, and that the Sovereign, who is no less than a collective being, cannot be represented except by himself: the power indeed may be transmitted, but not the will.

In reality, if it is not impossible for a particular will to agree on some point with the general will, it is at least impossible for the agreement to be lasting and constant; for the particular will tends, by its very nature, to partiality, while the general will tends to equality. It is even more impossible to have any guarantee of this agreement; for even if it should always exist, it would be the effect not of art, but of chance. The Sovereign may indeed say: "I now will actually what this man wills, or at least what he says he wills"; but it cannot say: "What he wills tomorrow, I too shall will" because it is absurd for the will to bind itself for the future, nor is it incumbent on any; will to consent to anything that is not for the good of the being who wills. If then the people promises simply to obey, by that very act it dissolves itself and loses what makes it a people; the moment a master exists, there is no longer a Sovereign, and from that moment the body politic has ceased to exist.

This does not mean that the commands of the rulers cannot pass for general wills, so long as the Sovereign, being free to oppose them, offers no opposition. In such a case, universal silence is taken to imply the consent of the people. This will be explained later on.

CHAPTER II: THAT SOVEREIGNTY IS INDIVISIBLE

Sovereignty, for the same reason as makes it inalienable, is indivisible; for will either is, or is not, general;[1] it is the will either of the body of the people, or only of a part of it. In the first case, the will, when declared, is an act of Sovereignty and constitutes law: in the second, it is merely a particular will, or act of magistracy—at the most a decree.

But our political theorists, unable to divide Sovereignty in principle, divide it according to its object: into force and will; into legislative power and executive power; into rights of taxation, justice and war; into internal administration and power of foreign treaty. Sometimes they confuse all these sections, and sometimes they distinguish them; they turn the Sovereign into a fantastic being composed of several connected pieces: it is

---

[1] To be general, a will need not always be unanimous; but every vote—must be counted: any exclusion is a breach of generality.

as if they were making man of several bodies, one with eyes, one with arms, another with feet, and each with nothing besides. We are told that the jugglers of Japan dismember a child before the eyes of the spectators; then they throw all the members into the air one after another, and the child falls down alive and whole. The conjuring tricks of our political theorists are very like that; they first dismember the body politic by an illusion worthy of a fair, and then join it together again we know not how.

This error is due to a lack of exact notions concerning the Sovereign authority, and to taking for parts of it what are only emanations from it. Thus, for example, the acts of declaring war and making peace have been regarded as acts of Sovereignty; but this is not the case, as these acts do not constitute law, but merely the application of a law, a particular act which decides how the law applies, as we shall see clearly when the idea attached to the word *law* has been defined.

If we examined the other divisions in the same manner, we should find that, whenever Sovereignty seems to be divided, there is an illusion: the rights which are taken as being part of Sovereignty are really all subordinate, and always imply supreme wills of which they only sanction the execution.

It would be impossible to estimate the obscurity this lack of exactness has thrown over the decisions of writers who have dealt with political right, when they have used the principles laid down by them to pass judgment on the respective rights of kings and peoples. Every one can see, in Chapters III and IV of the First Book of Grotius, how the learned man and his translator, Barbeyrac, entangle and tie themselves up in their own sophistries, for fear of saying too little or too much of what they think, and so offending the interests they have to conciliate. Grotius, a refugee in France, ill-content with his own country, and desirous of paying his court to Louis XIII, to whom his book is dedicated, spares no pains to rob the peoples of all their rights and invest kings with them by every conceivable artifice. This would also have been much to the taste of Barbeyrac, who dedicated his translation to George I of England. But unfortunately the expulsion of James II, which he called his "abdication," compelled him to use all reserve, to shuffle and to tergiversate, in order to avoid making William out a usurper. If these two writers had adopted the true principles, all difficulties would have been removed, and they would have been always consistent; but it would have been a sad truth for them to tell, and would have paid court for them to no-one save the people. Moreover, truth is no road to fortune, and the people dispenses neither ambassadorships, nor professorships, nor pensions.

CHAPTER III: WHETHER THE GENERAL WILL IS FALLIBLE

It follows from what has gone before that the general will is always right and tends to the public advantage; but it does not follow that the deliberations of the people are always equally correct. Our will is always for our own good, but we do not always see what that is; the people is never corrupted, but it is often deceived, and on such occasions only does it seem to will what is bad.

There is often a great deal of difference between the will of all and the general will; the latter considers only the common interest, while the former takes private interest into account, and is no more than a sum of particular wills: but take away from these same wills the pluses and minuses that cancel one another,[2] and the general will remains as the sum of the differences.

---

[2] "Every interest," says the Marquis d'Argenson, "has different principles. The

If, when the people, being furnished with adequate information, held its deliberations, the citizens had no communication one with another, the grand total of the small differences would always give the general will, and the decision would always be good. But when factions arise, and partial associations are formed at the expense of the great association, the will of each of these associations becomes general in relation to its members, while it remains particular in relation to the State: it may then be said that there are no longer as many votes as there are men, but only as many as there are associations. The differences become less numerous and give a less general result. Lastly, when one of these associations is so great as to prevail over all the rest, the result is no longer a sum of small differences, but a single difference; in this case there is no longer a general will, and the opinion which prevails is purely particular.

It is therefore essential, if the general will is to be able to express itself, that there should be no partial society within the State, and that each citizen should think only his own thoughts:[3] which was indeed the sublime and unique system established by the great Lycurgus. But if there are partial societies, it is best to have as many as possible and to prevent them from being unequal, as was done by Solon, Numa and Servius. These precautions are the only ones that can guarantee that the general will shall be always enlightened, and that the people shall in no way deceive itself.

CHAPTER IV: THE LIMITS OF THE SOVEREIGN POWER

If the State is a moral person whose life is in the union of its members, and if the most important of its cares is the care for its own preservation, it must have a universal and compelling force, in order to move and dispose each part as may be most advantageous to the whole. As nature gives each man absolute power over all his members, the social compact gives the body politic absolute power over all its members also; and it is this power which, under the direction of the general will, bears, as I have said, the name of Sovereignty.

But, besides the public person, we have to consider the private persons composing it, whose life and liberty are naturally independent of it. We are bound then to distinguish clearly between the respective rights of the citizens and the Sovereign,[4] and between the duties the former have to fulfil as subjects, and the natural rights they should enjoy as men.

Each man alienates, I admit, by the social compact, only such part of his powers, goods and liberty as it is important for the community to control; but it must also be granted that the Sovereign is sole judge of what is important.

---

agreement of two particular interests is formed by opposition to a third." He might have added that the agreement of all interests is formed by opposition to that of each. If there were no different interests, the common interest would be barely felt, as it would encounter no obstacle; all would go on of its own accord, and politics would cease to be an art.

[3] "In fact," says Macchiavelli, "there are some divisions that are harmful to a Republic and some that are advantageous. Those which stir up sects and parties are harmful; those attended by neither are advantageous. Since, then, the founder of a Republic cannot help enmities arising, he ought at least to prevent them from growing into sects" (*History of Florence,* Book vii). Rousseau quotes the Italian.

[4] Attentive readers, do not, I pray, be in a hurry to charge me with contradicting myself. The terminology made it unavoidable, considering the poverty of the language; but wait and see.

Every service a citizen can render the State he ought to render as soon as the Sovereign demands it; but the Sovereign, for its part, cannot impose upon its subjects any fetters that are useless to the community, nor can it even wish to do so; for no more by the law of reason than by the law of nature can anything occur without a cause.

The undertakings which bind us to the social body are obligatory only because they are mutual; and their nature is such that in fulfilling them we cannot work for others without working for ourselves. Why is it that the general will is always in the right, and that all continually will the happiness of each one, unless it is because there is not a man who does not think of "each" as meaning him, and consider himself in voting for all? This proves that equality of rights and the idea of justice which such equality creates originate in the preference each man gives to himself, and accordingly in the very nature of man. It proves that the general will, to be really such, must be general in its object as well as its essence; that it must both come from all and apply to all; and that it loses its natural rectitude when it is directed to some particular and determinate object, because in such a case we are judging of something foreign to us, and have no true principle of equity to guide us.

Indeed, as soon as a question of particular fact or right arises on a point not previously regulated by a general convention, the matter becomes contentions. It is a case in which the individuals concerned are one party, and the public the other, but in which I can see neither the law that ought to be followed nor the judge who ought to give the decision. In such a case, it would be absurd to propose to refer the question to an express decision of the general will, which can be only the conclusion reached by one of the parties and in consequence will be, for the other party, merely an external and particular will, inclined on this occasion to injustice and subject to error. Thus, just as a particular will cannot stand for the general will, the general will, in turn, changes its nature, when its object is particular, and, as general, cannot pronounce on a man or a fact. When, for instance, the people of Athens nominated or displaced its rulers, decreed honours to one, and imposed penalties on another, and, by a multitude of particular decrees, exercised all the functions of government indiscriminately, it had in such cases no longer a general will in the strict sense; it was acting no longer as Sovereign, but as magistrate. This will seem contrary to current views; but I must be given time to expound my own.

It should be seen from the foregoing that what makes the will general is less the number of voters than the common interest uniting them; for under this system, each necessarily submits to the conditions he imposes on others; and this admirable agreement between interest and justice gives to the common deliberations an equitable character which at once vanishes when any particular question is discussed, in the absence of a common interest to unite and identify the ruling of the judge with that of the party.

From whatever side we approach our principle, we reach the same conclusion, that the social compact sets up among the citizens an equality of such a kind, that they all bind themselves to observe the same conditions and should therefore all enjoy the same rights. Thus, from the very nature of the compact, every "act of Sovereignty", *i.e.* every authentic act of the general will, binds or favours all the citizens equally; so that the Sovereign recognises only the body of the nation, and draws no distinctions between those of whom it is made up. What, then, strictly speaking is an act of Sovereignty? It is not a convention between a superior and an inferior, but a convention between the body and each of its members. It is legitimate, because based on the social contract, and, equitable, because common to all; useful, because it can have no other object than the general good, and stable, because guaranteed by the public force and the supreme power. So long as the subjects have to submit only to conventions of this sort, they obey no-one but their own will; and to ask how far the respective rights of the Sovereign and the citizens extend, is to ask up to what point the latter can enter into undertakings with themselves, each with all, and all with each.

We can see from this that the sovereign power, absolute, sacred and inviolable as it is, does not and cannot exceed the limits of general conventions, and that every man may dispose at will of such goods and liberty as these conventions leave him; so that the Sovereign never has a right to lay more charges on one subject than on another, because, in that case, the question becomes particular, and ceases to be within its competency.

When these distinctions have once been admitted, it is seen to be so untrue that there is, in the social contract, any real renunciation on the part of the individuals, that the position in which they find themselves as a result of the contract is really preferable to that in which they were before. Instead of a renunciation, they have made an advantageous exchange: instead of an uncertain and precarious way of living they have got one that is better and more secure; instead of natural independence they have got liberty, instead of the power to harm others security for themselves, and instead of their strength, which others might overcome, a right which social union makes invincible. Their very life, which they have devoted to the State, is by it constantly protected; and when they risk it in the State's defence, what more are they doing than giving back what they have received from it? What are they doing that they would not do more often and with greater danger in the state of nature, in which they would inevitably have to fight battles at the peril of their lives in defence of that which is the means of their preservation? All have indeed to fight when their country needs them; but then no one has ever to fight for himself. Do we not gain something by running, on behalf of what gives us our security, only some of the risks we should have to run for ourselves, as soon as we lost it?

CHAPTER V: THE RIGHT OF LIFE AND DEATH

The question is often asked how individuals, having no right to dispose of their own lives, can transfer to the Sovereign a right which they do not possess. The difficulty of answering this question seems to me to lie in its being wrongly stated. Every man has a right to risk his own life in order to preserve it. Has it ever, been said that a man who throws himself out of the window to escape from a fire is guilty of suicide? Has such a crime ever been laid to the charge of him who perishes in a storm because, when he went on board, he knew of the danger?

The social treaty has for its end the preservation of the contracting parties. He who wills the end wills the means also, and the means must involve some risks, and even some losses. He who wishes to preserve his life at others expense should also, when it is necessary, be ready to give it up for their sake. Furthermore, the citizen is no longer the judge of the dangers to which the law desires him to expose himself; and when the prince says to him: "It is expedient for the State that you should die," he ought to die, because it is only on that condition that he has been living in security up to the present, and because his life is no longer a mere bounty of nature, but a gift made conditionally by the State.

The death-penalty inflicted upon criminals may be looked on in much the same light: it is in order that we may not fall victims to an assassin that we consent to die if we ourselves turn assassins. In this treaty, so far from disposing of our own lives, we think only of securing them, and it is not to be assumed that any of the parties then expects to get hanged.

Again, every malefactor, by attacking social rights, becomes on forfeit a rebel and a traitor to his country; by violating its laws he ceases to be a member of it; he even makes war upon it. In such a case the preservation of the State is inconsistent with his own, and one or the other must perish; in putting the guilty to death, we slay not so much the citizen as an enemy. The trial and the judgment are the proofs that he has broken the social treaty, and is in consequence no longer a member of the State. Since, then, he has recognised himself to be such by living there, he must be removed by exile as a violator of the compact, or by death as a public enemy; for such an enemy is not a moral person, but merely a man; and in such a case the right of war is to kill the vanquished.

But, it will be said, the condemnation of a criminal is a particular act. I admit it: but such condemnation is not a function of the Sovereign; it is a right the Sovereign can confer without being able itself to exert it. All my ideas are consistent, but I cannot expound them all at once.

We may add that frequent punishments are always a sign of weakness or remissness on the part of the government. There is not a single ill-doer who could not be turned to some good. The State has no right to put to death, even for the sake of making an example, any one whom it can leave alive without danger.

The right of pardoning or exempting the guilty from a penalty imposed by the law and pronounced by the judge belongs only to the authority which is superior to both judge and law, *i.e.* the Sovereign; even its right in this matter is far from clear, and the cases for exercising it are extremely rare. In a well-governed State, there are few punishments, not because there are many pardons, but because criminals are rare; it is when a State is in decay that the multitude of crimes is a guarantee of impunity. Under the Roman Republic, neither the Senate nor the Consuls ever attempted to pardon; even the people never did so, though it sometimes revoked its own decision. Frequent pardons mean that crime will soon need them no longer, and no-one can help seeing whither that leads. But I feel my heart protesting and restraining my pen; let us leave these questions to the just man who has never offended, and would himself stand in no-need of pardon.

CHAPTER VI: LAW

By the social compact we have given the body politic existence and life: we have now by legislation to give it movement and will. For the original act by which the body is formed and united still in no respect determines what it ought to do for its preservation.

What is well and in conformity with order is so by the nature of things and independently of human conventions. All justice comes from God, who is its sole source; but if we knew how to receive so high an inspiration, we should need neither government nor laws. Doubtless, there is a universal justice emanating from reason alone; but this justice, to be admitted among us, must be mutual. Humanly speaking, in default of natural sanctions, the laws of justice are ineffective among men: they merely make for the good of the wicked and the undoing of the just, when the just man observes them towards everybody and nobody observes them towards him. Conventions and laws are therefore needed to join rights to duties and refer justice to its object. In the state of nature, where everything is common, I owe nothing to him whom I have promised nothing; I recognise as belonging to others only what is of no use to me. In the state of society all rights are fixed by law, and the case becomes different.

But what, after all, is a law? As long as we remain satisfied with attaching purely metaphysical ideas to the word, we shall go on arguing without arriving at an understanding; and when we have defined a law of nature, we shall be no nearer the definition of a law of the State.

I have already said that there can be no general will directed to a particular object. Such an object must be either within or outside the State. If outside, a will which is alien to it cannot be, in relation to it, general; if within, it is part of the State, and in that case there arises a relation between whole and part which makes them two separate beings, of which the part is one, and the whole minus the part the other. But the whole minus a part cannot be the whole; and while this relation persists, there can be no whole, but only two unequal parts; and it follows that the will of one is no longer in any respect general in relation to the other.

But when the whole people decrees for the whole people, it is considering only itself; and if a relation is then formed, it is between two aspects of the entire object, without there being any division of the whole. In that case the matter about which the decree is made is, like the decreeing will general. This act is what I call a law.

When I say that the object of laws is always general, I mean that law considers subjects *en masse* and actions in the abstract, and never a particular person or action. Thus the law may indeed decree that there shall be privileges, but cannot confer them on anybody by name. It may set up several classes of citizens, and even lay down the qualifications for membership of these classes, but it cannot nominate such and such persons as belonging to them; it may establish a monarchical government and hereditary succession, but it cannot choose a king, or nominate a royal family. In a word, no function which has a particular object belongs to the legislative power.

On this view, we at once see that it can no longer be asked whose business it is to make laws, since they are acts of the general will: nor whether the prince is above the law, since he is a member of the State; nor whether the law can be unjust, since no one is unjust to himself; nor how we can be both free and subject to the laws since they are but registers of our wills.

We see further that, as the law unites universality of will with universality of object, what a man, whoever he be, commands of his own motion cannot be a law; and even what the Sovereign commands with regard to a particular matter is no nearer being a law, but is a decree, an act, not of sovereignty, but of magistracy.

I therefore give the name 'Republic' to every State that is governed by laws, no matter what the form of its administration may be: for only in such a case does the public interest govern, and the *res publica* rank as a *reality*. Every legitimate government is republican;[5] what government is I will explain later on.

Laws are, properly speaking, only the conditions of civil association. The people, being subject to the laws, ought to be their author: the conditions of the society ought to be regulated solely by those who come together to form it. But how are they to regulate them? Is it to be by common agreement, by a sudden inspiration? Has the body politic an organ to declare its will? Who can give it the foresight to formulate and announce its acts in advance? Or how is it to announce them in the hour of need? How can a blind multitude, which often does not know what it wills, because it rarely knows what is good for it, carry out for itself so great and difficult an enterprise as a system of legislation? Of itself the people wills always the good, but of itself it by no means always sees it. The general will is always in the right, but the judgment which guides it is not always enlightened. It must be got to see objects as they are, and sometimes as they ought to appear to it; it must be shown the good road it is in search of, secured from the seductive influences of individual wills, taught to see times and spaces as a series, and made to weigh the attractions of present and sensible advantages against the danger of distant and hidden evils. The individuals see the good they reject; the public wills the good it does not see. All stand equally in need of guidance. The former must be compelled to bring their wills into conformity with their reason; the latter must be taught to know what it

---

[5] I understand by this word, not merely an aristocracy or a democracy, but generally any government directed by the general will, which is the law. To be legitimate, the government must be, not one with the Sovereign, but its minister. In such a case even a monarchy is a Republic. This will be made clearer in the following book.

wills. If that is done, public enlightenment leads to the union of understanding and will in the social body: the parts are made to work exactly together, and the whole is raised to its highest power. This makes a legislator necessary.

CHAPTER VII: THE LEGISLATOR

In order to discover the rules of society best suited to nations, a superior intelligence beholding all the passions of men without experiencing any of them would be needed. This intelligence would have to be wholly unrelated to our nature, while knowing it through and through; its happiness would have to be independent of us, and yet ready to occupy itself with ours; and lastly, it would have, in the march of time, to look forward to a distant glory, and, working in one century, to be able to enjoy in the next.[6] It would take gods to give men laws.

What Caligula argued from the facts, Plato, in the dialogue called the *Politicus*, argued in defining the civil or kingly man, on the basis of right. But if great princes are rare, how much more so are great legislators? The former have only to follow the pattern which the latter have to lay down. The legislator is the engineer who invents the machine, the prince merely the mechanic who sets it up and makes it go. "At the birth of societies," says Montesquieu, "the rulers of Republics establish institutions, and afterwards the institutions mould the rulers."[7]

He who dares to undertake the making of a people's institutions ought to feel himself capable, so to speak, of changing human nature, of transforming each individual, who is by himself a complete and solitary whole, into part of a greater whole from which he in a manner receives his life and being; of altering man's constitution for the purpose of strengthening it; and of substituting a partial and moral existence for the physical and independent existence nature has conferred on us all. He must, in a word, take away from man his own resources and give him instead new ones alien to him, and incapable of being made use of without the help of other men. The more completely these natural resources are annihilated, the greater and the more lasting are those which he acquires, and the more stable and perfect the new institutions; so that if each citizen is nothing and can do nothing without the rest, and the resources acquired by the whole are equal or superior to the aggregate of the resources of all the individuals, it may be said that legislation is at the highest possible point of perfection.

The legislator occupies in every respect an extraordinary position in the State. If he should do so by reason of his genius, he does so no less by reason of his office, which is neither magistracy, nor Sovereignty. This office, which sets up the Republic, nowhere enters into its constitution; it is an individual and superior function, which has nothing in common with human empire; for if he who holds command over men ought not to have command over the laws, he who has command over the laws ought not any more to have it over men; or else his laws would be the ministers of his passions and would often merely serve to perpetuate his injustices: his private aims would inevitably mar the sanctity of his work.

When Lycurgus gave laws to his country, he began by resigning the throne. It was the custom of most Greek towns to entrust the establishment of their laws to foreigners. The Republics of modern Italy in many cases followed this example; Geneva did the

---

[6] A people becomes famous only when its legislation begins to decline. We do not know for how many centuries the system of Lycurgus made the Spartans happy before the rest of Greece took any notice of it.

[7] Montesquieu, *The Greatness and Decadence of the Romans*, ch. i.

same and profited by it.[8] Rome, when it was most prosperous, suffered a revival of all the crimes of tyranny, and was brought to the verge of destruction, because it put the legislative authority and the sovereign power into the same hands.

Nevertheless, the decemvirs themselves never claimed the right to pass any law merely on their own authority. "Nothing we propose to you," they said to the people, "can pass into law without your consent. Romans, be yourselves the authors of the laws which are to make you happy."

He, therefore, who draws up the laws has, or should have, no right of legislation, and the people cannot, even if it wishes, deprive itself of this incommunicable right, because, according to the fundamental compact, only the general will can bind the individuals, and there can be no assurance that a particular will is in conformity with the general will, until it has been put to the free vote of the people. This I have said already; but it is worth while to repeat it.

Thus in the task of legislation we find together two things which appear to be incompatible: an enterprise too difficult for human powers, and, for its execution, an authority that is no authority.

There is a further difficulty that deserves attention. Wise men, if they try to speak their language to the common herd instead of its own, cannot possibly make themselves understood. There are a thousand kinds of ideas which it is impossible to translate into popular language. Conceptions that are too general and objects that are too remote are equally out of its range: each individual, having no taste for any other plan of government than that which suits his particular interest, finds it difficult to realise the advantages he might hope to draw from the continual privations good laws impose. For a young people to be able to relish sound principles of political theory and follow the fundamental rules of statecraft, the effect would have to become the cause; the social spirit, which should be created by these institutions, would have to preside over their very foundation; and men would have to be before law what they should become by means of law. The legislator therefore, being unable to appeal to either force or reason, must have recourse to an authority of a different order capable of constraining without violence and persuading without convincing.

This is what has, in all ages, compelled the fathers of nations to have recourse to divine intervention and credit the gods with their own wisdom, in order that the peoples, submitting to the laws of the State as to those of nature, and recognising the same power in the formation of the city as in that of man, might obey freely, and bear with docility the yoke of the public happiness.

This sublime reason, far above the range of the common herd, is that whose decisions the legislator puts into the mouth of the immortals, in order to constrain by divine authority those whom human prudence could not move.[9] But it is not anybody who can make the gods speak, or get himself believed when he proclaims himself their interpreter. The great soul of the legislator is the only miracle that can prove his mission.

---

[8] Those who know Calvin only as a theologian much underestimate the extent of his genius. The codification of our wise edicts, in which he played a large part, does him no less honour than his *Institute*. Whatever revolution time may bring in our religion, so long as the spirit of patriotism and liberty still lives among us, the memory of this great man will be for ever blessed.

[9] "In truth," says Macchiavelli, "there has never been, in any country, an extraordinary legislator who has not had recourse to God; for otherwise his laws would not have been accepted: there are, in fact, many useful truths of which a wise man may have knowledge without their having in themselves such clear reasons for their being so as to be able to convince others" (*Discourses on Livy*, Bk. v, ch. xi). (Rousseau quotes the Italian.)

Any man may grave tablets of stone, or buy an oracle; or feign secret intercourse with some divinity, or train a bird to whisper in his ear, or find other vulgar ways of imposing on the people. He whose knowledge goes no further may perhaps gather round him a band of fools; but he will never found an empire, and his extravagances will quickly perish with him. Idle tricks form a passing tie; only wisdom can make it lasting. The Judaic law, which still subsists, and that of the child of Ishmael, which, for ten centuries, has ruled half the world, still proclaim the great men who laid them down; and, while the pride of philosophy or the blind spirit of faction sees in them no more than lucky impostures, the true political theorist admires, in the institutions they set up, the great and powerful genius which presides over things made to endure.

We should not, with Warburton, conclude from this that politics and religion have among us a common object, but that, in the first periods of nations, the one is used as an instrument for the other.

CHAPTER VIII: THE PEOPLE

As, before putting up a large building, the architect surveys and sounds the site to see if it will bear the weight, the wise legislator does not begin by laying down laws good in themselves, but by investigating the fitness of the people, for which they are destined, to receive them. Plato refused to legislate for the Arcadians and the Cyrenæans, because he knew that both peoples were rich and could not put up with equality; and good laws and bad men were found together in Crete, because Minos had inflicted discipline on a people already burdened with vice.

A thousand nations have achieved earthly greatness, that could never have endured good laws; even such as could have endured them could have done so only for a very brief period of their long history. Most peoples, like most men, are docile only in youth; as they grow old they become incorrigible. When once customs have become established and prejudices inveterate, it is dangerous and useless to attempt their reformation; the people, like the foolish and cowardly patients who rave at sight of the doctor, can no longer bear that any one should lay hands on its faults to remedy them.

There are indeed times in the history of States when, just as some kinds of illness turn men's heads and make them forget the past, periods of violence and revolutions do to peoples what these crises do to individuals: horror of the past takes the place of forgetfulness, and the State, set on fire by civil wars, is born again, so to speak, from its ashes, and takes on anew, fresh from the jaws of death, the vigour of youth. Such were Sparta at the time of Lycurgus, Rome after the Tarquins, and, in modern times, Holland and Switzerland after the expulsion of the tyrants.

But such events are rare; they are exceptions, the cause of which is always to be found in the particular constitution of the State concerned. They cannot even happen twice to the same people, for it can make itself free as long as it remains barbarous, but not when the civic impulse has lost its vigour. Then disturbances may destroy it, but revolutions cannot mend it: it needs a master, and not a liberator. Free peoples, be mindful of maxim; "Liberty may be gained, but can never be recovered."

Youth is not infancy. There is for nations, as for men, a period of youth, or, shall we say, maturity, before which they should not be made subject to laws; but the maturity of a people is not always easily recognisable, and, if it is anticipated, the work is spoilt. One people is amenable to discipline from the beginning; another, not after ten centuries. Russia will never be really civilised, because it was civilised too soon. Peter had a genius for imitation; but he lacked true genius, which is creative and makes all from nothing. He did some good things, but most of what he did was out of place. He saw that his people was barbarous, but did not see that it was not ripe for civilisation: he wanted to civilise it when it needed only hardening. His first wish was to make Germans or Englishmen, when he ought to have been making Russians; and he prevented his subjects from ever becoming what they might have been by persuading them that they were what they are not. In this fashion too, a French teacher turns out his pupil to be an infant prodigy, and for the rest of his life to be nothing whatsoever. The empire of Russia will aspire to conquer Europe, and will itself be conquered. The Tartars, its subjects or neighbours, will become its masters and ours, by a revolution which I regard as inevitable. Indeed, all the kings of Europe are working in concert to hasten its coming.

CHAPTER IX: THE PEOPLE (*continued*)

As nature has set bounds to the stature of a well-made man, and, outside those limits, makes nothing but giants or dwarfs, similarly, for the constitution of a State to be at its best, it is possible to fix limits that will make it neither too large for good government, nor too small for self-maintenance. In every body politic there is a *maximum* strength which it cannot exceed and which it only loses by increasing in size. Every extension of the social tie means its relaxation; and, generally speaking, a small State is stronger in proportion than a great one.

A thousand arguments could be advanced in favour of this principle. First, long distances make administration more difficult, just as a weight becomes heavier at the end of a longer lever. Administration therefore becomes more and more burdensome as the distance grows greater; for, in the first place, each city has its own, which is paid for by the people: each district its own, still paid for by the people: then comes each province, and then the great governments, satrapies, and vice-royalties, always costing more the higher you go, and always at the expense of the unfortunate people. Last of all comes the supreme administration, which eclipses all the rest. All these overcharges are a continual drain upon the subjects; so far from being better governed by all these different orders, they are worse governed than if there were only a single authority over them. In the meantime, there scarce remain resources enough to meet emergencies; and, when recourse must be had to these, the State is always on the eve of destruction.

This is not all; not only has the government less vigour and promptitude for securing the observance of the laws, preventing nuisances, correcting abuses, and guarding against seditious undertakings begun in distant places; the people has less affection for its rulers, whom it never sees, for its country, which, to its eyes, seems like the world, and for its fellow-citizens, most of whom are unknown to it. The same laws cannot suit so many diverse provinces with different customs, situated in the most various climates, and incapable of enduring a uniform government. Different laws lead only to trouble and confusion among peoples which, living under the same rulers and in constant communication one with another, intermingle and intermarry, and, coming under the sway of new customs, never know if they can call their very patrimony their own. Talent is buried, virtue unknown and vice unpunished, among such a multitude of men who do not know one another, gathered together in one place at the seat of the central administration. The leaders, overwhelmed with business, see nothing for themselves; the State is governed by clerks. Finally, the measures which have to be taken to, maintain the general authority, which all these distant officials wish to escape or to impose upon, absorb all the energy of the public, so that there is none left for the happiness of the people. There is hardly enough to defend it when need arises, and thus a body which is too big for its constitution gives way and falls crushed under its own weight.

Again, the State must assure itself a safe foundation, if it is to have stability, and to be able to resist the shocks it cannot help experiencing, as well as the efforts it will be forced to make for its maintenance; for all peoples have a kind of centrifugal force that makes them continually act one against another, and tend to aggrandise themselves at their neighbours' expense, like the vortices of Descartes. Thus the weak run the risk of being soon swallowed up; and it is almost impossible for any one to preserve itself except by putting itself in a state of equilibrium with all, so that the pressure is on all sides practically equal.

It may therefore be seen that there are reasons for expansion and reasons for contraction; and it is no small part of the statesman's skill to hit between them the mean that is most favourable to the preservation of the State. It may be said that the reason for expansion, being merely external and relative, ought to be subordinate to the reasons for contraction, which are internal and absolute. A strong and healthy constitution is the first thing to look for; and it is better to count on the vigour which comes of good government than on the resources a great territory furnishes.

It may be added that there have been known States so constituted that the necessity of making conquests entered into their very constitution, and that, in order to maintain themselves, they were forced to expand ceaselessly. It may be that they congratulated themselves greatly on this fortunate necessity, which none the less indicated to them, along with the limits of their greatness, the inevitable moment of their fall.

CHAPTER X: THE PEOPLE (*continued*)

A body politic may be measured in two ways—either by the extent of its territory, or by the number of its people; and there is, between these two measurements, a right relation which makes the State really great. The men make the State, and the territory sustains the men; the right relation therefore is that the land should suffice for the maintenance of the inhabitants, and that there should be as many inhabitants as the land can maintain. In this proportion lies the *maximum* strength of a given number of people; for if there is too much land, it is troublesome to guard and inadequately cultivated, produces more than is needed, and soon gives rise to wars of defence; if there is not enough, the State depends on its neighbours for what it needs over and above, and this soon gives rise to wars of offence. Every people, to which its situation gives no choice save that between commerce and war, is weak in itself: it depends on its neighbours, and on circumstances; its existence can never be more than short and uncertain. It either conquers others, and changes its situation, or it is conquered and becomes nothing. Only insignificance or greatness can keep it free.

No fixed relation can be stated between the extent of \: territory and the population that are adequate one to the other, both because of the differences in the quality of land, in its fertility, in the nature of its products, and in the influence of climate, and because of the different tempers of those who inhabit it; for some in a fertile country consume little, and others on an ungrateful soil much. The greater or less fecundity of women, the conditions that are more or less favourable in each country to the growth of population, and the influence the legislator can hope to exercise by his institutions, must also be taken into account. The legislator therefore should not go by what he sees, but by what he foresees; he should stop not so much at the state in which he actually finds the population, as at that to which it ought naturally to attain. Lastly, there are countless cases in which the particular local circumstances demand or allow the acquisition of a greater territory than seems necessary. Thus, expansion will be great in a mountainous country, where the natural products, *i.e.* woods and pastures, need less labour, where we know from experience that women are more fertile than in the plains, and where a great expanse of slope affords only a small level tract that can be counted on for vegetation. On the other hand, contraction is possible on the coast, even in lands of rocks and nearly barren sands, because there fishing makes up to a great extent for the lack of land-produce, because the inhabitants have to congregate together more in order to repel pirates, and further because it is easier to unburden die country of its superfluous inhabitants by means of colonies.

To these conditions of law-giving must be added one other which, though it cannot take the place of the rest, renders them all useless when it is absent. This is the enjoyment of peace and plenty; for the moment at which a State sets its house in order is, like the moment when a battalion is forming up, that when its body is least capable of offering resistance and easiest to destroy. A better resistance could be made at a time of absolute disorganisation than at a moment of fermentation, when each is occupied with his own position and not with the danger. If war, famine, or sedition arises at this time of crisis, the State will inevitably be overthrown.

Not that many governments have not been set up during such storms; but in such cases these governments are themselves the State's destroyers. Usurpers always bring about or select troublous times to get passed, under cover of the public terror, destructive laws, which the people would never adopt in cold blood. The moment chosen is one of the surest means of distinguishing the work of the legislator from that of the tyrant.

What people, then, is a fit subject for legislation? One which, already bound by some unity of origin, interest, or convention, has never yet felt the real yoke of law; one that has neither customs nor superstitions deeply ingrained, one which stands in no fear of being overwhelmed by sudden invasion; one which, without entering into its neighbours' quarrels, can resist each of them single-handed, or get the help of one to repel another; one in which every member may be known by every other, and there is no need to lay on any man burdens too heavy for a man to bear; one which can do without other peoples, and without which all others can do;[10] one which is neither rich nor poor, but self-sufficient; and, lastly, one which unites the consistency of an ancient people with the docility of a new one. Legislation is made difficult less by what it is necessary to build up than by what has to be destroyed; and what makes success so rare is the impossibility of finding natural simplicity together with social requirements. All these conditions are indeed rarely found united, and therefore few States have good constitutions.

There is still in Europe one country capable of being given laws—Corsica. The valour and persistency with which that brave people has regained and defended its liberty well deserves that some wise man should teach it how to preserve what it has won. I have a feeling that some day that little island will astonish Europe.

CHAPTER XI: THE VARIOUS SYSTEMS OF LEGISLATION

If we ask in what precisely consists the greatest good of all, which should be the end of every system of legislation, we shall find it reduce itself to two main objects, liberty and equality—liberty, because all particular dependence means so much force taken from the body of the State, and equality, because liberty cannot exist without it.

---

[10] If there were two neighbouring peoples, one of which could not do without the other, it would be very hard on the former, and very dangerous for the latter. Every wise nation, in such a case, would make haste to free the other from dependence. The Republic of Thlascala, enclosed by the Mexican Empire, preferred doing without salt to buying from the Mexicans, or even getting it from them as a gift The Thlascalans were wise enough to see the snare hidden under such liberality. They kept their freedom, and that little State, shut up in that great Empire, was finally the instrument of its ruin.

I have already defined civil liberty; by equality, we should understand, not that the degrees of power and riches are to be absolutely identical for everybody; but that power shall never be great enough for violence, and shall always be exercised by virtue of rank and law; and that, in respect of riches, no citizen shall ever be wealthy enough to buy another, and none poor enough to be forced to sell himself:[11] which implies, on the part of the great, moderation in goods and position, and, on the side of the common sort, moderation in avarice and covetousness.

Such equality, we are told, is an unpractical ideal that cannot actually exist. But if its abuse is inevitable, does it follow that we should not at least make regulations concerning it? It is precisely because the force of circumstances tends continually to destroy equality that the force of legislation should always tend to its maintenance.

But these general objects of every good legislative system need modifying in every country in accordance with the local situation and the temper of the inhabitants; and these circumstances should determine, in each case, the particular system of institutions which is best, not perhaps in itself, but for the State for which it is destined. If, for instance, the soil is barren and unproductive, or the land too crowded for its inhabitants, the people should turn to industry and the crafts, and exchange what they produce for the commodities they lack. If, on the other hand, a people dwells in rich plains and fertile slopes, or, in a good land, lacks inhabitants, it should give all its attention to agriculture, which causes men to multiply, and should drive out the crafts, which would only result in depopulation, by grouping in a few localities the few inhabitants there are.[12] If a nation dwells on an extensive and convenient coast-line, let it cover the sea with ships and foster commerce and navigation. It will have a life that will be short and glorious. If, on its coasts, the sea washes nothing but almost inaccessible rocks, let it remain barbarous and ichthyophagous: it will have a quieter, perhaps a better, and certainly a happier life. In a word, besides the principles that are common to all, every nation has in itself something that gives them a particular application, and makes its legislation peculiarly its own. Thus, among the Jews long ago and more recently among the Arabs, the chief object was religion, among the Athenians letters, at Carthage and Tyre commerce, at Rhodes shipping, at Sparta war, at Rome virtue. The author of *The Spirit of the Laws* has shown with many examples by what art the legislator directs the constitution towards each of these objects.

What makes the constitution of a State really solid and lasting is the due observance of what is proper, so that the natural relations are always in agreement with the laws on every point, and law only serves, so to speak, to assure, accompany and rectify them. But if the legislator mistakes his object and adopts a principle other than circumstances naturally direct; if his principle makes for servitude while they make for liberty, or if it makes for riches, while they make for populousness, or if it makes for peace, while they make for conquest—the laws will insensibly lose their influence, the constitution will alter, and the State will have no rest from trouble till it is either destroyed or changed, and nature has resumed her invincible sway.

---

[11] If the object is to give the State consistency, bring the two extremes as near to each other as possible; allow neither rich men nor beggars. These two estates, which are naturally inseparable, are equally fatal to the common good; from the one come the friends of tyranny, and from the other tyrants. It is always between them that public liberty is put up to auction; the one buys, and the other sells.

[12] "Any branch of foreign commerce," says M. d'Argenson, "creates on the whole only apparent advantage for the kingdom in general; it may enrich some individuals, or even some towns; but the nation as a whole gains nothing by it, and the people is no better off."

CHAPTER XII: THE DIVISION OF THE LAWS

If the whole is to be set in order, and the commonwealth put into the best possible shape, there are various relations to be considered. First, there is the action of the complete body upon itself, the relation of the whole to the whole, of the Sovereign to the State; and this relation, as we shall see, is made up of the relations of the intermediate terms.

The laws which regulate this relation bear the name of political laws, and are also called fundamental laws, not without reason if they are wise. For, if there is, in each State, only one good system, the people that is in possession of it should hold fast to this; but if the established order is bad, why should laws that prevent men from being good be regarded as fundamental? Besides, in any case, a people is always in a position to change its laws, however good; for, if it choose to do itself harm, who can have a right to stop it?

The second relation is that of the members one to another, or to the body as a whole; and this relation should be in the first respect as unimportant, and in the second as important, as possible. Each citizen would then be perfectly independent of all the rest, and at the same time very dependent on the city; which is brought about always by the same means, as the strength of the State can alone secure the liberty of its members. From this second relation arise civil laws.

We may consider also a third kind of relation between the individual and the law, a relation of disobedience to its penalty. This gives rise to the setting up of criminal laws, which, at bottom, are less a particular class of law than the sanction behind all the rest.

Along with these three kinds of law goes a fourth, most important of all, which is not graven on tablets of marble or brass, but on the hearts of the citizens. This forms the real constitution of the State, takes on every day new powers, when other laws decay or die out, restores them or takes their place, keeps a people in the ways in which it was meant to go, and insensibly replaces authority by the force of habit. I am speaking of morality, of custom, above all of public opinion; a power unknown to political thinkers, on which none the less success in everything else depends. With this the great legislator concerns himself in secret, though he seems to confine himself to particular regulations; for these are only the arc of the arch, while manners and morals, slower to arise, form in the end its immovable keystone.

Among the different classes of laws, the political, which determine the form of the government, are alone relevant to my subject.

BOOK III

Before speaking of the different forms of government, let us try to fix the exact sense of the word, which has not yet been very clearly explained.

CHAPTER I: GOVERNMENT IN GENERAL

I warn the reader that this chapter requires careful reading, and that I am unable to make myself clear to those who refuse to be attentive.

Every free action is produced by the concurrence of two causes; one moral, *i.e.* the will which determines the act; the other physical, *i.e.* the power which executes it. When I walk towards an object, it is necessary first that I should will to go there, and, in the second place, that my feet should carry me. If a paralytic wills to run and an active man wills not to, they will both stay where they are. The body politic has the same motive powers; here too force and will are distinguished, will under the name of legislative power and force under that of executive power. Without their concurrence, nothing is, or should be, done.

We have seen that the legislative power belongs to the people, and can belong to it alone. It may, on the other hand, readily be seen, from the principles laid down above, that the executive power cannot belong to the generality as legislature or Sovereign, because it consists wholly of particular acts which fall outside the competency of the law, and consequently of the Sovereign, whose acts must always be laws.

The public force therefore needs an agent of its own to bind it together and set it to work under the direction of the general will, to serve as a means of communication between the State and the Sovereign, and to do for the collective person more or less what the union of soul and body does for man. Here we have what is, in the State, the basis of government, often wrongly confused with the Sovereign, whose minister it is.

What then is government? An intermediate body set up between the subjects and the Sovereign, to secure their mutual correspondence, charged with the execution of the laws and the maintenance of liberty, both civil and political.

The members of this body are called magistrates or *kings*, that is to say *governors*, and the whole body bears the name *prince*.[1] Thus those who hold that the act, by which a people puts itself under a prince, is not a contract, are certainly right. It is simply and solely a commission, an employment, in which the rulers, mere officials of the Sovereign, exercise in their own name the power of which it makes them depositaries. This power it can limit, modify or recover at pleasure; for the alienation of such a right is incompatible with the nature of the social body, and contrary to the end of association.

I call then *government*, or supreme administration, the legitimate exercise of the executive power, and prince or magistrate the man or the body entrusted with that administration.

In government reside the intermediate forces whose relations make up that of the whole to the whole, or of the Sovereign to the State. This last relation may be represented as that between the extreme terms of a continuous proportion, which has government as its mean proportional. The government gets from the Sovereign the orders it gives the people, and, for the State to be properly balanced, there must, when everything is reckoned in, be equality between the product or power of the government taken in itself,

---

[1] Thus at Venice the College, even in the absence of the Doge, is called "Most Serene Prince."

and the product or power of the citizens, who are on the one hand sovereign and on the other subject.

Furthermore, none of these three terms can be altered without the equality being instantly destroyed. If the Sovereign desires to govern, or the magistrate to give laws, or if the subjects refuse to obey, disorder takes the place of regularity, force and will no longer act together, and the State is dissolved and falls into despotism or anarchy. Lastly, as there is only one mean proportional between each relation, there is also only one good government possible for a State. But, as countless events may change the relations of a people, not only may different governments be good for different peoples, but also for the same people at different times.

In attempting to give some idea of the various relations that may hold between these two extreme terms, I shall take as an example the number of a people, which is the most easily expressible.

Suppose the State is composed of ten thousand citizens. The Sovereign can only be considered collectively and as a body; but each member, as being a subject, is regarded as an individual: thus the Sovereign is to the subject as ten thousand to one, *i.e.* each member of the State has as his share only a ten-thousandth part of the sovereign authority, although he is wholly under its control. If the people numbers a hundred thousand, the condition of the subject undergoes no change, and each equally is under the whole authority of the laws, while his vote, being reduced to one hundred thousandth part, has ten times less influence in drawing them up. The subject therefore remaining always a unit, the relation between him and the Sovereign increases with the number of the citizens. From this it follows that, the larger the State, the less the liberty.

When I say the relation increases, I mean that it grows more unequal. Thus the greater it is in the geometrical sense, the less relation there is in the ordinary sense of the word. In the former sense, the relation, considered according to quantity, is expressed by the quotient; in the latter, considered according to identity, it is reckoned by similarity.

Now, the less relation the particular wills have to the general will, that is, morals and manners to laws, the more should the repressive force be increased. The government, then, to be good, should be proportionately stronger as the people is more numerous.

On the other hand, as the growth of the State gives the depositaries of the public authority more temptations and chances of abusing their power, the greater the force with which the government ought to be endowed for keeping the people in hand, the greater too should be the force at the disposal of the Sovereign for keeping the government in hand. I am speaking, not of absolute force, but of the relative force of the different parts of the State.

It follows from this double relation that the continuous proportion between the Sovereign, the prince and the people, is by no means an arbitrary idea, but a necessary consequence of the nature of the body politic. It follows further that, one of the extreme terms, viz. the people, as subject, being fixed and represented by unity, whenever the duplicate ratio increases or diminishes, the simple ratio does the same, and is changed accordingly. From this we see that there is not a single unique and absolute form of government, but as many governments differing in nature as there are States differing in size.

If, ridiculing this system, any one were to say that, in order to find the mean proportional and give form to the body of the government, it is only necessary, according to me, to find the square root of the number of the people, I should answer that I am here taking this number only as an instance; that the relations of which I am speaking are not measured by the number of men alone, but generally by the amount of action, which is a combination of a multitude of causes; and that, further, if, to save words, I borrow for a moment the terms of geometry, I am none the less well aware that moral quantities do not allow of geometrical accuracy.

The government is on a small scale what the body politic which includes it is on a great one. It is a moral person endowed with certain faculties, active like the Sovereign and passive like the State, and capable of being resolved into other similar relations. This accordingly gives rise to a new proportion, within which there is yet another, according to the arrangement of the magistracies, till an indivisible middle term is reached, *i.e.* a single ruler or supreme magistrate, who may be represented, in the midst of this progression, as the unity between the fractional and the ordinal series.

Without encumbering ourselves with this multiplication of terms, let us rest content with regarding government as a new body within the State, distinct from the people and the Sovereign, and intermediate between them.

There is between these two bodies this essential difference, that the State exists by itself, and the government only through the Sovereign. Thus the dominant will of the prince is, or should be, nothing but the general will or the law; his force is only the public force concentrated in his hands, and, as soon as he tries to base any absolute and independent act on his own authority, the tie that binds the whole together begins to be loosened. If finally the prince should come to have a particular will more active than the will of the Sovereign, and should employ the public force in his hands in obedience to this particular will, there would be, so to speak, two Sovereigns, one rightful and the other actual, the social union would evaporate instantly, and the body politic would be dissolved.

However, in order that the government may have a true existence and a real life distinguishing it from the body of the State, and in order that all its members may be able to act in concert and fulfil the end for which it was set up, it must have a particular personality, a sensibility common to its members, and a force and will of its own making for its preservation. This particular existence implies assemblies, councils, power of deliberation and decision, rights, titles, and privileges belonging exclusively to the prince and making the office of magistrate more honourable in proportion as it is more troublesome. The difficulties lie in the manner of so ordering this subordinate whole within the whole, that it in no way alters the general constitution by affirmation of its own, and always distinguishes the particular force it possesses, which is destined to aid in its preservation, from the public force, which is destined to the preservation of the State; and, in a word, is always ready to sacrifice the government to the people, and never to sacrifice the people to the government.

Furthermore, although the artificial body of the government is the work of another artificial body, and has, we may say, only a borrowed and subordinate life, this does not prevent it from being able to act with more or less vigour or promptitude, or from being, so to speak, in more or less robust health. Finally, without departing directly from the end for which it was instituted, it may deviate more or less from it, according to the manner of its constitution.

From all these differences arise the various relations which the government ought to bear to the body of the State, according to the accidental and particular relations by which the State itself is modified, for often the government that is best in itself will become the most pernicious, if the relations in which it stands have altered according to the defects of the body politic to which it belongs.

CHAPTER II: THE CONSTITUENT PRINCIPLE IN THE VARIOUS FORMS OF GOVERNMENT

To set forth the general cause of the above differences, we must here distinguish between government and its principle, as we did before between the State and the Sovereign.

The body of the magistrate may be composed of a greater or a less number of members. We said that the relation of the Sovereign to the subjects was greater in proportion as the people was more numerous, and, by a clear analogy, we may say the same of the relation of the government to the magistrates.

But the total force of the government, being always that of the State, is invariable; so that, the more of this force it expends on its own members, the less it has left to employ on the whole people.

The more numerous the magistrates, therefore, the weaker the government. This principle being fundamental, we must do our best to make it clear.

In the person of the magistrate we can distinguish three essentially different wills: first, the private will of the individual, tending only to his personal advantage; secondly, the common will of the magistrates, which is relative solely to the advantage of the prince, and may be called corporate will, being general in relation to the government, and particular in relation to the State, of which the government forms part; and, in the third place, the will of the people or the sovereign will, which is general both in relation to the State regarded as the whole, and to the government regarded as a part of the whole.

In a perfect act of legislation, the individual or particular will should be at zero; the corporate will belonging to the government should occupy a very subordinate position; and, consequently, the general or sovereign will should always predominate and should be the sole guide of all the rest.

According to the natural order, on the other hand, these different wills become more active in proportion as they are concentrated. Thus, the general will is always the weakest, the corporate will second, and the individual will strongest of all: so that, in the government, each member is first of all himself, then a magistrate, and then a citizen —in an order exactly the reverse of what the social system requires.

This granted, if the whole government is in the hands of one man, the particular and the corporate will are wholly united, and consequently the latter is at its highest possible degree of intensity. But, as the use to which the force Is put depends on the degree reached by the will, and as the absolute force of the government is invariable, it follows that the most active government is that of one man.

Suppose, on the other hand, we unite the government with the legislative authority, and make the Sovereign prince also, and all the citizens so many magistrates: then the corporate will, being confounded with the general will, can possess no greater activity than that will, and must leave the particular will as strong as it can possibly be. Thus, the government, having always the same absolute force, will be at the lowest point of its relative force or activity.

These relations are incontestable, and there are other considerations which still further confirm them. We can see, for instance, that each magistrate is more active in the body to which he belongs than each citizen in that to which he belongs, and that consequently the particular will has much more influence on the acts of the government than on those of the Sovereign; for each magistrate is almost always charged with some governmental function, while each citizen, taken singly, exercises no function of Sovereignty. Furthermore, the bigger the State grows, the more its real force increases, though not in direct proportion to its growth; but, the State remaining the same, the number of magistrates may increase to any extent, without the government gaining any greater real force; for its force is that of the State, the dimension of which remains equal. Thus the relative force or activity of the government decreases, while its absolute or real force cannot increase.

Moreover, it is a certainty that promptitude in execution diminishes as more people are put in charge of it: where prudence is made too much of, not enough is made of fortune; opportunity is let slip, and deliberation results in the loss of its object.

I have just proved that the government grows remiss in proportion as the number of the magistrates increases; and I previously proved that, the more numerous the people, the greater should be the repressive force. From this it follows that the relation of the magistrates to the government should vary inversely to the relation of the subjects to the Sovereign; that is to say, the larger the State, the more should the government be tightened, so that the number of the rulers diminish in proportion to the increase of that of the people.

It should be added that I am here speaking of the relative strength of the government, and not of its rectitude: for, on the other hand, the more numerous the magistracy, the nearer the corporate will comes to the general will; while, under a single magistrate, the corporate will is, as I said, merely a particular will. Thus, what may be gained on one side is lost on the other, and the art of the legislator is to know how to fix the point at which the force and the will of the government, which are always in inverse proportion, meet in the relation that is most to the advantage of the State.

CHAPTER III: THE DIVISION OF GOVERNMENTS

We saw in the last chapter what causes the various kinds or forms of government to be distinguished according to the number of the members composing them: it remains in this to discover how the division is made.

In the first place, the Sovereign may commit the charge of the government to the whole people or to the majority of the people, so that more citizens are magistrates than are mere private individuals. This form of government is called *democracy*.

Or it may restrict the government to a small number; so that there are more private citizens than magistrates; and this is named *aristocracy*.

Lastly, it may concentrate the whole government in the hands of a single magistrate from whom all others hold their power. This third form is the most usual, and is called *monarchy*, or royal government.

It should be remarked that all these forms, or at least the first two, admit of degree, and even of very wide differences; for democracy may include the whole people, or may be restricted to half. Aristocracy, in its turn, may be restricted indefinitely from half the people down to the smallest possible number. Even royalty is susceptible of a measure of distribution. Sparta always had two kings, as its constitution provided; and the Roman Empire saw as many as eight emperors at once, without it being possible to say that the Empire was split up. Thus there is a point at which each form of government passes into the next, and it becomes clear that, under three comprehensive denominations, government is really susceptible of as many diverse forms as the State has citizens.

There are even more: for, as the government may also, in certain aspects, be subdivided into other parts, one administered in one fashion and one in another, the combination of the three forms may result in a multitude of mixed forms, each of which admits of multiplication by all the simple forms.

There has been at all times much dispute concerning the best form of government, without consideration of the fact that each is in some cases the best, and in others the worst.

If, in the different States, the number of supreme magistrates should be in inverse ratio to the number of citizens, it follows that, generally, democratic government suits small States, aristocratic government those of middle size, and monarchy great ones. This rule is immediately deducible from the principle laid down. But it is impossible to count the innumerable circumstances which may furnish exceptions.

CHAPTER IV: DEMOCRACY

He who makes the law knows better than any one else how it should be executed and interpreted. It seems then impossible to have a better constitution than that in which the executive and legislative powers are united; but this very fact renders the government in certain respects inadequate, because things which should be distinguished are confounded, and the prince and the Sovereign, being the same person, form, so to speak, no more than a government without government.

It is not good for him who makes the laws to execute them, or for the body of the people to turn its attention away from a general standpoint and devote it to particular objects. Nothing is more dangerous than the influence of private interests in public affairs, and the abuse of the laws by the government is a less evil than the corruption of the legislator, which is the inevitable sequel to a particular standpoint. In such a case, the State being altered in substance, all reformation becomes impossible. A people that would never misuse governmental powers would never misuse independence; a people that would always govern well would not need to be governed.

If we take the term in the strict sense, there never has been a real democracy, and there never will be. It is against the natural order for the many to govern and the few to be governed. It is unimaginable that the people should remain continually assembled to devote their time to public affairs, and it is clear that they cannot set up commissions for that purpose without the form of administration being changed.

In fact, I can confidently lay down as a principle that, when the functions of government are shared by several tribunals, the less numerous sooner or later acquire the greatest authority, if only because they are in a position to expedite affairs, and power thus naturally comes into their hands.

Besides, how many conditions that are difficult to unite does such a government presuppose! First, a very small State, where the people can readily be got together and where each citizen can with ease know all the rest; secondly, great simplicity of manners, to prevent business from multiplying and raising thorny problems; next, a large measure of equality in rank and fortune, without which equality of rights and authority cannot long subsist; lastly, little or no luxury—for luxury either comes of riches or makes them necessary; it corrupts at once rich and poor, the rich by possession and the poor by covetousness; it sells the country to softness and vanity, and takes away from the State all its citizens, to make them slaves one to another, and one and all to public opinion.

This is why a famous writer has made virtue the fundamental principle of Republics; for all these conditions could not exist without virtue. But, for want of the necessary distinctions, that great thinker was often inexact, and sometimes obscure, and did not see that, the sovereign authority being everywhere the same, the same principle should be found in every well-constituted State, in a greater or less degree, it is true, according to the form of the government.

It may be added that there is no government so subject to civil wars and intestine agitations as democratic or popular government, because there is none which has so strong and continual a tendency to change to another form, or which demands more vigilance and courage for its maintenance as it is. Under such a constitution above all, the citizen should arm himself with strength and constancy, and say, every day of his life, what a virtuous Count Palatine[2] said in the Diet of Poland: Malo periculosam libertatem quam quietum servitium.

Were there a people of gods, their government would be democratic. So perfect a government is not for men.

CHAPTER V: ARISTOCRACY

We have here two quite distinct moral persons, the government and the Sovereign, and in consequence two general wills, one general in relation to all the citizens, the other only for the members of the administration. Thus, although the government may regulate its internal policy as it pleases, it can never speak to the people save in the name of the Sovereign, that is, of the people itself, a fact which must not be forgotten.

The first societies governed themselves aristocratically. The heads of families took counsel together on public affairs. The young bowed without question to the authority of experience. Hence such names as *priests, elders, senate,* and *gerontes.* The savages of North America govern themselves in this way even now, and their government is admirable.

But, in proportion as artificial inequality produced by institutions became predominant over natural inequality, riches or power[3] were put before age, and aristocracy became elective. Finally, the transmission of the father's power along with his goods to his children, by creating patrician families, made government hereditary, and there came to be senators of twenty.

There are then three sorts of aristocracy—natural, elective and hereditary. The first is only for simple peoples; the third is the worst of all governments; the second is the best, and is aristocracy properly so called.

Besides the advantage that lies in the distinction between the two powers, it presents that of its members being chosen; for, in popular government, all the citizens are born magistrates; but here magistracy is confined to a few, who become such only by election.[4] By this means uprightness, understanding, experience and all other claims to pre-eminence and public esteem become so many further guarantees of wise government.

Moreover, assemblies are more easily held, affairs better discussed and carried out with more order and diligence, and the credit of the State is better sustained abroad by venerable senators than by a multitude that is unknown or despised.

---

[2] The Palatine of Posen, father of the King of Poland, Duke of Lorraine. I prefer liberty with danger to peace with slavery.

[3] It is clear that the word *optimates* meant, among the ancients, not the best, but the most powerful.

[4] It is of great importance that the form of the election of magistrates should be regulated by law; for if it is left at the discretion of the prince, k is impossible to avoid falling into hereditary aristocracy, as the Republics of Venice and Berne actually did. The first of these has therefore long been a State dissolved; the second, however, is maintained by the extreme wisdom of the senate, and forms an honourable and highly dangerous exception.

In a word, it is the best and most natural arrangement that the wisest should govern the many, when it is assured that they will govern for its profit, and not for their own. There is no need to multiply instruments, or get twenty thousand men to do what a hundred picked men can do even better, but it must not be forgotten mat corporate interest here begins to direct the public power less under the regulation of the general will, and that a further inevitable propensity takes away from the laws part of the executive power.

If we are to speak of what is individually desirable, neither should the State be so small, nor a people so simple and upright, that the execution of the laws follows immediately from the public will, as it does in a good democracy. Nor should the nation be so great that the rulers have to scatter in order to govern it and are able to play the Sovereign each in his own department, and, beginning by making themselves independent, end by becoming masters.

But if aristocracy does not demand all the virtues needed by popular government, it demands others which are peculiar to itself; for instance, moderation on the side of the rich and contentment on that of the poor; for it seems that thorough-going equality would be out of place, as it was not found even at Sparta.

Furthermore, if this form of government carries with it a certain inequality of fortune, this is justifiable in order that as a rule the administration of public affairs may be entrusted to those who are most able to give them their whole time, but not, as Aristotle maintains, in order that the rich may always be put first. On the contrary, it is of importance that an opposite choice should occasionally teach the people that the deserts of men offer claims to pre-eminence more important than those of riches.

CHAPTER VI: MONARCHY

So far, we have considered the prince as a moral and collective person, unified by the force of the laws, and the depositary in the State of the executive power. We have now to consider this power when it is gathered together into the hands of a natural person, a rear man, who alone has the right to dispose of it in accordance with the laws. Such a person is called a monarch or king.

In contrast with other forms of administration, in which a collective being stands for an individual, in this form an individual stands for a collective being; so that the moral unity that constituted the prince is at the same time a physical unity, and all the qualities, which in the other case are only with difficulty brought together by the law, are found naturally united.

Thus the will of the people, the will of the prince, the public force of the State, and the particular force of the government, all answer to a single motive power; all the springs of the machine are in the same hands, the whole moves towards the same end; there are no conflicting movements to cancel one another, and no kind of constitution can be imagined in which a less amount of effort produces a more considerable amount of action. Archimedes, seated quietly on the bank and easily drawing a great vessel afloat, stands to my mind for a skilful monarch, governing vast states from his study, and moving everything while he seems himself unmoved.

But if no government is more vigorous than this, there is also none in which the particular will holds more sway and rules the rest more easily. Everything moves towards the same end indeed, but this end is by no means that of the public happiness, and even the force of the administration constantly shows itself prejudicial to the State.

Kings desire to be absolute, and men are always crying out to them from afar that the best means of being so is to get themselves loved by their people. This precept is all very well, and even in some respects very true. Unfortunately, it will always be derided at court. The power which comes of a people's love is no doubt the greatest; but it is precarious and conditional, and princes will never rest content with it. The best kings desire to be in a position to be wicked, if they please, without forfeiting their mastery: political sermonisers may tell them to their hearts' content that, the people's strength being their own, their first interest is that the people should be prosperous, numerous and formidable; they are well aware that this is Untrue. Their first personal interest is that the people should be weak, wretched, and unable to resist them. I admit that, provided the subjects remained always in submission, the prince's interest would indeed be that it should be powerful, in order that its power, being his own, might make him formidable to his neighbours; but, this interest being merely secondary and subordinate, and strength being incompatible with submission, princes naturally give the preference always to the principle that is more to their immediate advantage. This is what Samuel put strongly before the Hebrews, and what Macchiavelli has clearly shown. He professed to teach kings; but it was the people he really taught. His *Prince* is the book of Republicans.[5]

We found, on general grounds, that monarchy is suitable only for great States, and this is confirmed when we examine it in itself. The more numerous the public administration, the smaller becomes the relation between the prince and the subjects, and the nearer it comes to equality, so that in democracy the ratio is unity, or absolute equality. Again, as the government is restricted in numbers the ratio increases and reaches its *maximum* when the government is in the hands of a single person. There is then too great a distance between prince and people and the State lacks a bond of union. To form such a bond, there must be intermediate orders, and princes, personages and nobility to compose them. But no such things suit a small State, to which all class differences mean ruin.

If, however, it is hard for a great State to be well governed, it is much harder for it to be so by a single man; and every one knows what happens when kings substitute others for themselves.

An essential and inevitable defect, which will always rank monarchical below republican government, is that in a republic the public voice hardly ever raises to the highest positions men who are not enlightened and capable, and such as to fill them with honour; while in monarchies these who rise to the top are most often merely petty blunderers petty swindlers, and petty intriguers, whose petty talents cause them to get into the highest positions at Court, but, as soon as they have got there, serve only to make their ineptitude clear to the public. The people is far less often mistaken in its choice than the prince; and a man of real worth among the king's ministers is almost as rare as a fool at the head of a republican government. Thus, when, by some fortunate chance, one of these born governors takes the helm of State in some monarchy that has been nearly overwhelmed by swarms of 'gentlemanly' administrators, there is nothing but amazement at the resources he discovers, and his coming marks an era in his country's history.

For a monarchical State to have a chance of being well governed, its population and extent must be proportionate to the abilities of its governor. If is easier to conquer than to

---

[5] Macchiavelli was a proper man and a good citizen; but, being attached to the court of the Medici, he could not help veiling his love of liberty in the midst of his country's oppression. The choice of his detestable hero, Cæsar Borgia, clearly enough shows his hidden aim; and the contradiction between the teaching of the *Prince* and that of the *Discourses on Livy* and the *History of Florence* shows that this profound political thinker has so far been studied only by superficial or corrupt readers. The Court of Rome sternly prohibited his book. I can well believe it; for it is that Court it most clearly portrays.

rule. With a long enough lever, the world could be moved with a single finger; to sustain it needs the shoulders of Hercules. However small a State may be, the prince is hardly ever big enough for it. When, on the other hand, it happens that the State is too small for its ruler, in these rare cases too it is ill governed, because the ruler, constantly pursuing his great designs, forgets the interests of the people, and makes it no less wretched by misusing the talents he has, than a ruler of less capacity would make it for want of those he had not. A kingdom should, so to speak, expand or contract with each reign, according to the prince's capabilities; but, the abilities of a senate being more constant in quantity, the State can then have permanent frontiers without the administration suffering.

The disadvantage that is most felt in monarchical government is the want of the continuous succession which, in both the other forms, provides an unbroken bond of union. When one king dies, another is needed; elections leave dangerous intervals and are full of storms; and unless the citizens are disinterested and upright to a degree which very seldom goes with this kind of government, intrigue and corruption abound. He to whom the State has sold itself can hardly help selling it in his turn and repaying himself, at the expense of the weak, the money the powerful have wrung from him. Under such an administration, venality sooner or later spreads through every part, and peace so enjoyed under a king is worse than the disorders of an interregnum.

What has been done to prevent these evils? Crowns have been made hereditary in certain families, and an order of succession has been set up, to prevent disputes from arising on the death of kings. That is to say, the disadvantages of regency have been put in place of those of election, apparent tranquillity has been preferred to wise administration, and men have chosen rather to risk having children, monstrosities, or imbeciles as rulers to having disputes over the choice of good kings. It has not been taken into account that, in so exposing ourselves to the risks this possibility entails, we are setting almost all the chances against us. There was sound sense in what the younger Dionysius said to his father, who reproached him for doing some shameful deed by asking, "Did I set you the example?" "No," answered his son, "but your father was not king."

Everything conspires to take away from a man who is set in authority over others the sense of justice and reason. Much trouble, we are told, is taken to teach young princes the art of reigning; but their education seems to do them no good. It would be better to begin by teaching them the art of obeying. The greatest kings whose praises history tells were not brought up to reign: reigning is a science we are never so far from possessing as when we have learnt too much of it, and one we acquire better by obeying than by commanding. "Nam utilissimus idem ac brevissimus bonarum malarumque rerum delectus cogitare quid aut nolueris sub alio principe, aut volueris."[6]

One result Of this lack of coherence is the inconstancy of royal government, which, regulated now on one scheme and now on another, according to the character of the reigning prince or those who reign for him, cannot for long have a fixed object or a consistent policy—and this variability, not found in the other forms of government, where the prince is always the same, causes the State to be always shifting from principle to principle and from project to project. Thus we may say that generally, if a court is more subtle in intrigue, there is more wisdom in a senate, and Republics advance towards their ends by more consistent and better considered policies; while every revolution in a royal ministry creates a revolution in the State; for the principle common to all ministers

---

[6] Tacitus, *Histories*, i. 16. "For the best, and also the shortest way of finding out what is good and what is bad is to consider what you would have wished to happen or not to happen, had another than you been Emperor."

and nearly all kings is to do in every respect the reverse of what was done by their predecessors.

This incoherence further clears up a sophism that is very familiar to royalist political writers; not only is civil government likened to domestic government, and the prince to the father of a family—this error has already been refuted—but the prince is also freely credited with all the virtues he ought to possess, and is supposed to be always what he should be. This supposition once made, royal government is clearly preferable to all others, because it is incontestably the strongest, and, to be the best also, wants only a corporate will more in conformity with the general will.

But if, according to Plato,[7] the "king by nature" is such a rarity, how often will nature and fortune conspire to give him a crown? And, if royal education necessarily corrupts those who receive it, what is to be hoped from a series of men brought up to reign? It is, then, wanton self-deception to confuse royal government with government by a good king. To see such government as it is in itself, we must consider it as it is under princes who are incompetent or wicked: for either they will come to the throne wicked or incompetent, or the throne will make them so.

These difficulties have not escaped our writers, who, all the same, are not troubled by them. The remedy, they say, is to obey without a murmur: God sends bad kings in His wrath, and they must be borne as the scourges of Heaven. Such talk is doubtless edifying; but it would be more in place in a pulpit than in a political book. What are we to think of a doctor who promises miracles, and whose whole art is to exhort the sufferer to patience? We know for ourselves that we must put up with a bad government when it is there; the question is how to find a good one.

CHAPTER VII: MIXED GOVERNMENTS

Strictly speaking, there is no such thing as a simple government. An isolated ruler must have subordinate magistrates; a popular government must have a head. There is therefore, in the distribution of the executive power, always a gradation from the greater to the lesser number, with the difference that sometimes the greater number is dependent on the smaller, and sometimes the smaller on the greater.

Sometimes the distribution is equal, when either the constituent parts are in mutual dependence, as in the government of England, or the authority of each section is independent, but imperfect, as in Poland. This last form is bad; for it secures no unity in the government, and the State is left without a bond of union.

Is a simple or a mixed government the better? Political writers are always debating the question, which must be answered as we have already answered a question about all forms of government.

Simple government is better in itself, just because it is simple. But when the executive power is not sufficiently dependent upon the legislative power, *i.e.* when the prince is more closely related to the Sovereign than the people to the prince, this lack of proportion must be cured by the division of the government; for all the parts have then no less authority over the subjects, while their division makes them all together less strong against the Sovereign.

The same disadvantage is also prevented by the appointment of intermediate magistrates, who leave the government entire, and have the effect only of balancing the two powers and maintaining their respective rights. Government is then not mixed, but moderated.

---

[7] In the *Politicus*.

The opposite disadvantages may be similarly cured, and, when the government is too lax, tribunals may be set up to concentrate it. This is done in all democracies. In the first case, the government is divided to make it weak; in the second, to make it strong: for the *maxima* of both strength and weakness are found in simple governments, while the mixed forms result in a mean strength.

CHAPTER VIII: THAT ALL FORMS OF GOVERNMENT DO NOT SUIT ALL COUNTRIES

Liberty not being a fruit of all climates, is not within the reach of all peoples. The more this principle, laid down by Montesquieu, is considered, the more its truth is felt; the more it is combated, the more chance is given to confirm it by new proofs.

In all the governments that there are, the public person consumes without producing. Whence then does it get what it consumes? From the labour of its members. The necessities of the public are supplied out of the superfluities of individuals. It follows that the civil State can subsist only so long as men's labour brings them a return greater than their needs.

The amount of this excess is not the same in all countries. In some it is considerable, in others middling, in yet others nil, in some even negative. The relation of product to subsistence depends on the fertility of the climate, on the sort of labour the land demands, on the nature of its products, on the strength of its inhabitants, on the greater or less consumption they find necessary, and on several further considerations of which the whole relation is made up.

On the other side, all governments are not of the same nature: some are less voracious than others, and the differences between them are based on this second principle, that the further from their source the public contributions are removed, the more burdensome they become.

The charge should be measured not by the amount of the impositions, but by the path they have to travel in order to get back to those from whom they came. When the circulation is prompt and well-established, it does not matter whether much or little is paid; the people is always rich and, financially speaking, all is well. On the contrary, however little the people gives, if that little does not return to it, it is soon exhausted by giving continually: the State is then never rich, and the people is always a people of beggars.

It follows that, the more the distance between people and government increases, the more burdensome tribute becomes: thus, in a democracy, the people bears the least charge; in an aristocracy, a greater charge; and, in monarchy, the weight becomes heaviest. Monarchy therefore suits only wealthy nations; aristocracy, States of middling size and wealth; and democracy, States that are small and poor.

In fact, the more we reflect, the more we find the difference between free and monarchical States to be this: in the former, everything is used for the public advantage; in the latter, the public forces and those of individuals are affected by each other, and either increases as the other grows weak; finally, instead of governing subjects to make them happy, despotism makes them wretched in order to govern them.

We find then, in every climate, natural causes according to which the form of government which it requires can be assigned, and we can even say what sort of inhabitants it should have.

Unfriendly and barren lands, where the product does; not repay the labour, should remain desert and uncultivated, or peopled only by savages; lands where men's labour brings in no more than the exact *minimum* necessary to subsistence should be inhabited by barbarous peoples: in such places all polity is impossible. Lands where the surplus of product over labour is only middling are suitable for free peoples; those in which the soil is abundant and fertile and gives a great product for a little labour call for monarchical government, in order that the surplus of superfluities among the subjects may be consumed by the luxury of the prince: for it is better for this excess to be absorbed by the government than dissipated among the individuals. I am aware that there are exceptions; but these exceptions themselves confirm the rule, in that sooner or later they produce revolutions which restore things to the natural order.

General laws should always be distinguished from individual causes that may modify their effects. If all the South were covered with Republics and all the North with despotic States, it would be none the less true that, in point of climate, despotism is suitable to hot countries, barbarism to cold countries, and good polity to temperate regions. I see also that, the principle being granted, there may be disputes on its application; it may be said that there are cold countries that are very fertile, and tropical countries that are very unproductive. But this difficulty exists only for those who do not consider the question in all its aspects. We must, as I have already said, take labour, strength, consumption, etc., into account.

Take two tracts of equal extent, one of which brings in five and the other ten. If the inhabitants of the first consume four and those of the second nine, the surplus of the first product will be a fifth and that of the second a tenth. The ratio of these two surpluses will then be inverse to that of the products, and the tract which produces only five will give a surplus double that of the tract which produces ten.

But there is no question of a double product, and I think no one would put the fertility of cold countries, as a general rule, on an equality with that of hot ones. Let us, however, suppose this equality to exist: let us, if you will, regard England as on the same level as Sicily, and Poland as Egypt—further south, we shall have Africa and the Indies; further north, nothing at all. To get this equality of product, what a difference there must be in tillage: in Sicily, there is only need to scratch the ground; in England, haw men must toil! But, where more hands are needed to get the same product, the superfluity must necessarily be less.

Consider, besides, that the same number of men consume much less in hot countries. The climate requires sobriety for the sake of health; and Europeans who try to live there as they would at home all perish of dysentery and indigestion. "We are," says Chardin, "carnivorous animals, wolves, in comparison with the Asiatics. Some attribute the sobriety of the Persians to the fact that their country is less cultivated; but it is my belief that their country abounds less in commodities because the inhabitants need less. If their frugality," he goes on, "were the effect of the nakedness of die land, only the poor would eat little; but everybody does so. Again, less or more would be eaten in various provinces, according to the land's fertility; but the same sobriety is found throughout the kingdom. They are very proud of their manner of life, saying that you have only to look at their hue to recognise how far it excels that of the Christians. In fact, the Persians are of an even hue; their skins are fair, fine and smooth; while die hue of their subjects, the Armenians, who live after the European fashion, is rough and blotchy, and their bodies are gross and unwieldy."

The nearer you get to the equator, the less people live on. Meat they hardly touch; rice, maize, curcur, millet and cassava are their ordinary food. There are in the Indies millions of men whose subsistence does not cost a halfpenny a day. Even in Europe we find considerable differences of appetite between Northern and Southern peoples. A

Spaniard will live for a week on a German's dinner. In the countries in which men are more voracious, luxury therefore turns in the direction of consumption. In England, luxury appears in a well-filled table; in Italy, you feast on sugar and flowers.

Luxury in clothes shows similar differences. In climates in which the changes of season are prompt and violent, men have better and simpler clothes; where they clothe themselves only for adornment, what is striking is more thought of than what is useful; clothes themselves are then a luxury. At Naples, you may see daily walking in the Pausilippeum men in gold-embroidered upper garments and nothing else. It is the same with buildings; magnificence is the sole consideration where there is nothing to fear from the air. In Paris and London, you desire to be lodged warmly and comfortably; in Madrid, you have superb salons, but not a window that closes, and you go to bed in a mere hole.

In hot countries foods are much more substantial and succulent; and the third difference cannot but have an influence on the second. Why are so many vegetables eaten in Italy? Because there they are good, nutritious and excellent in taste. In France, where they are nourished only on water, they are far from nutritious and are thought nothing of at table. They take up all the same no less ground, and cost at least as much pains to cultivate. It is a proved fact that the wheat of Barbary, in other respects inferior to that of France, yields much more flour, and that the wheat of France in turn yields more than that of northern countries; from which it may be inferred that a like gradation in the same direction, from equator to pole, is found generally. But is it not an obvious disadvantage for an equal product to contain less nourishment?

To all these points may be added another, which at once depends on and strengthens them. Hot countries need inhabitants less than cold countries, and can support more of them. There is thus a double surplus, which is all to the advantage of despotism. The greater the territory occupied by a fixed number of inhabitants, the more difficult revolt becomes, because rapid or secret concerted action is impossible, and the government can easily unmask projects and cut communications; but the more a numerous people is gathered together, the less can the government usurp the Sovereign's place: the people's leaders can deliberate as safely in their houses as the prince in council, and the crowd gathers as rapidly in the squares as the prince's troops in their quarters. The advantage of tyrannical government therefore lies in acting at great distances. With the help of the rallying-points it establishes, its strength, like that of the lever,[8] grows with distance. The strength of the people, on the other hand, acts only when concentrated: when spread abroad, it evaporates and is lost, like powder scattered on the ground, which catches fire only grain by grain. The least populous countries are thus the fittest for tyranny: fierce animals reign only in deserts.

CHAPTER IX: THE MARKS OF A GOOD GOVERNMENT

The question "What absolutely is the best government?" is unanswerable as well as indeterminate; or rather, there are as many good answers as there are possible combinations in the absolute and relative situations of all nations.

---

[8] This does not contradict what I said before (Book ii, ch. ix) about the disadvantages of great States; for we were then dealing with the authority of the government over the members, while here we are dealing with its force against the subjects. Its scattered members serve it as rallying-points for action against the people at a distance, but it has no rallying-point for direct action on its members themselves. Thus the length of the lever is its weakness in the one case, and its strength in the other.

But if it is asked by what sign we may know that a given people is well or ill governed, that is another matter, and the question, being one of fact, admits of an answer.

It is not, however, answered, because every-one wants to answer it in his own way. Subjects extol public tranquillity, citizens individual liberty; the one class prefers security of possessions, the other that of person; the one regards as the best government that which is most severe, the other maintains that the mildest is the best; the one wants crimes punished, the other wants them prevented; the one wants the State to be feared by its neighbours, the other prefers that it should be ignored; the one is content if money circulates, the other demands that the people shall have bread. Even if an agreement were come to on these and similar points, should we have got any further? As moral qualities do not admit of exact measurement, agreement about the mark does not mean agreement about the valuation.

For my part, I am continually astonished that a mark so simple is not recognised, or that men are of so bad faith as not to admit it. What is the end of political association? The preservation and prosperity of its members. And what is the surest mark of their preservation and prosperity? Their numbers and population. Seek then nowhere else this mark that is in dispute. The rest being equal, the government under which, without external aids, without naturalisation or colonies, the citizens increase and multiply most, is beyond question the best. The government under which a people wanes and diminishes is worst. Calculators, it is left for you to count, to measure, to compare.[9]

---

[9] On the same principle it should be judged what centuries deserve the preference for human prosperity. Those in which letters and arts have flourished have been too much admired, because the hidden object of their culture has not been fathomed, and their fatal effects not taken into account. "Idque apud imperitos humanitas vocabatur, cum pars servitutis esset." ["Fools called 'humanity' what was a part of slavery," Tacitus, *Agricola*, 31.] Shall we never see in the maxims books lay down the vulgar interest that makes their writers speak? No, whatever they may say, when, despite its renown, a country is depopulated, it is not true that all is well, and it is not enough that a poet should have an income of 100,000 francs to make his age the best of all. Less attention should be paid to the apparent repose and tranquillity of the rulers than to the well-being of their nations as wholes, and above all of the most numerous States. A hail-storm lays several cantons waste, but it rarely makes a famine. Outbreaks and civil wars give rulers rude shocks, but they are not the real ills of peoples, who may even get a respite, while there is a dispute as to who shall tyrannise over them. Their true prosperity and calamities come from their permanent condition: it is when the whole remains crushed beneath the yoke, that decay sets in, and that the rulers destroy them at will, and "ubi solitudinem faciunt, pacem appellant" ["Where they create solitude, they call it peace," Tacitus, *Agricola*, 31.] When the bickerings of the great disturbed the kingdom of France, and the Coadjutor of Paris took a dagger in his pocket to the Parliament, these things did not prevent the people of France from prospering and multiplying in dignity, ease and freedom. Long ago Greece flourished in the midst of the most savage wars; blood ran in torrents, and yet the whole country was covered with inhabitants. It appeared, says Macchiavelli, that in the midst of murder, proscription and civil war, our republic only throve: the virtue, morality and independence of the citizens did more to strengthen it than all their dissensions had done to enfeeble it A little disturbance gives the soul elasticity; what makes the race truly prosperous is not so much peace as liberty.

CHAPTER X: THE ABUSE OF GOVERNMENT AND ITS TENDENCY TO DEGENERATE

As the particular will acts constantly in opposition to the general will, the government continually exerts itself against the Sovereignty. The greater this exertion becomes, the more the constitution changes; and, as there is in this case no other corporate will to create an equilibrium by resisting the will of the prince, sooner or later the prince must inevitably suppress the Sovereign and break the social treaty. This is the unavoidable and inherent defect which, from the very birth of the body politic, tends ceaselessly to destroy it, as age and death end by destroying the human body.

There are two general courses by which government degenerates: *i.e.* when it undergoes contraction, or when the State is dissolved.

Government undergoes contraction when it passes from the many to the few, that is, from democracy to aristocracy, and from aristocracy to royalty. To do so is its natural propensity.[10] If it took the backward course from the few to the many, it could be said that it was relaxed; by this inverse sequence is impossible.

Indeed, governments never change their form except when their energy is exhausted and leaves them too weak to keep what they have. If a government at once extended its

---

[10] The slow formation and the progress of the Republic of Venice in its lagoons are a notable instance of this sequence; and it is most astonishing that, after more than twelve hundred years' existence, the Venetians seem to be still at the second stage, which they reached with the *Serrar di Consiglio* in 1198. As for the ancient Dukes who are brought up against them, it is proved, whatever the *Squittinio della libertà veneta* may say of them, that they were in no sense Sovereigns.

A case certain to be cited against my view is that of the Roman Republic, which, it will be said, followed exactly the opposite course, and passed from monarchy to aristocracy and from aristocracy to democracy. I by no means take this view of it.

What Romulus first set up was a mixed government, which soon deteriorated into despotism. From special causes, the State died an untimely death, as new-born children sometimes perish without reaching manhood. The expulsion of the Tarquins was the real period of the birth of the Republic. But at first it took on no constant form, because, by not abolishing the patriciate, it left half its work undone. For, by this means, hereditary aristocracy, the worst of all legitimate forms of administration, remained in conflict with democracy, and the form of the government, as Macchiavelli has proved, was only fixed on the establishment of the tribunate: only then was there a true government and a veritable democracy. In fact, the people was then not only Sovereign, but also magistrate and judge; the senate was only a subordinate tribunal, to temper and concentrate the government, and the consuls themselves, though they were patricians, first magistrates, and absolute generals in war, were in Rome itself no more than presidents of the people.

From that point, the government followed its natural tendency, and inclined strongly to aristocracy. The patriciate, we may say, abolished itself, and the aristocracy was found no longer in the body of patricians as at Venice and Genoa, but in the body of the senate, which was composed of patricians and plebeians, and even in the body of tribunes when they began to usurp an active function: for names do not affect facts, and, when the people has rulers who govern for it, whatever name they bear, the government is an aristocracy.

The abuse of aristocracy led to the civil wars and the triumvirate. Sulla, Julius Cæsar and Augustus became in fact real monarchs; and finally, under the despotism of Tiberius, the State was dissolved. Roman history then confirms, instead of invalidating, the principle I have laid down.

sphere and relaxed its stringency, its force would become absolutely nil, and it would persist still less. It is therefore necessary to wind up the spring and tighten the hold as it gives way: or else the State it sustains will come to grief.

The dissolution of the State may come about in either of two ways.

First, when the prince ceases to administer the State in accordance with the laws, and usurps the Sovereign power. A remarkable change then occurs: not the government, but the State, undergoes contraction; I mean that the great State is dissolved, and another is formed within it, composed solely of the members of the government, which becomes for the rest of the people merely master and tyrant. So that the moment the government usurps the Sovereignty, the social compact is broken and all private citizens recover by right their natural liberty, and are forced, but not bound, to obey.

The same thing happens when the members of the government severally usurp the power they should exercise only as a body; this is as great an infraction of the laws, and results in even greater disorders. There are then, so to speak, as many princes as there are magistrates, and the State, no less divided than the government, either perishes or changes its form.

When the State is dissolved, the abuse of government, whatever it is, bears the common name of *anarchy*. To distinguish, democracy degenerates into *ochlocracy* and aristocracy into *oligarchy* and I would add that royalty degenerates into *tyranny*; but this last word is ambiguous and needs explanation.

In vulgar usage, a tyrant is a king who governs violently and without regard for justice and law. In the exact sense, a tyrant is an individual who arrogates to himself the royal authority without having a right to it. This is how the Greeks understood the word "tyrant": they applied it indifferently to good and bad princes whose authority was not legitimate.[11] *Tyrant* and *usurper* are thus perfectly synonymous terms.

In order that I may give different things different names, I call him who usurps the royal authority *tyrant*, and him who usurps the sovereign power a *despot*. The tyrant is he who thrusts himself in contrary to the laws to govern in accordance with the laws; the despot is he who sets himself above the laws themselves. Thus the tyrant cannot be a despot, but the despot is always a tyrant.

CHAPTER XI: THE DEATH OF THE BODY POLITIC

Such is the natural and inevitable tendency of the best constituted governments. If Sparta and Rome perished, what State can hope to endure for ever? If we would set up a long-lived form of government, let us not even dream of making it eternal. If we are to succeed, we must not attempt the impossible, or flatter ourselves that we are endowing the work of man with a stability of which human conditions do not permit.

---

[11] Omnes enim et habentur et dicuntur tyranni, qui potestate utuntur perpetua in ea civitate quæ libertate usa est (Cornelius Nepos, *Life of Miltiades*). [For all those are called and considered tyrants, who hold perpetual power in a State that has known liberty.] It is true that Aristotle (*Nicomachean Ethics*, Book viii, chapter x) distinguishes the tyrant from the king by the fact that the former governs in his own interest, and the latter only for the good of his subjects; but not only did all Greek authors in general use the word *tyrant* in a different sense, as appears most clearly in Xenophon's *Hiero*, but also it would follow from Aristotle's distinction that, from the very beginning of the world, there has not yet been a single king.

The body politic, as well as the human body, begins to die as soon as it is born, and carries in itself the causes of its destruction. But both may have a constitution that is more or less robust and suited to preserve them a longer or a shorter time. The constitution of man is the work of nature; that of the State the work of art. It is not in men's power to prolong their own lives; but it is for them to prolong as much as possible the life of the State, by giving it the best possible constitution. The best constituted State will have an end; but it will end later than any other, unless some unforeseen accident brings about its untimely destruction.

The life-principle of the body politic lies in the sovereign authority. The legislative power is the heart of the State; the executive power is its brain, which causes the movement of all the parts. The brain may become paralysed and the individual still live. A man may remain an imbecile and live; but as soon as the heart ceases to perform its functions, the animal is dead.

The State subsists by means not of the laws, but of the legislative power. Yesterday's law is not binding to-day; but silence is taken for tacit consent, and the Sovereign is held to confirm incessantly the laws it does not abrogate as it might. All that it has once declared itself to will it wills always, unless it revokes its declaration.

Why then is so much respect paid to old laws? For this very reason. We must believe that nothing but the excellence of old acts of will can have preserved them so long: if the Sovereign had not recognised them as throughout salutary, it would have revoked them a thousand times. This is why, so far from growing weak, the laws continually gain new strength in any well constituted State; the precedent of antiquity makes them daily more venerable: while wherever the laws grow weak as they become old, this proves that there is no longer a legislative power, and that the State is dead.

CHAPTER XII: HOW THE SOVEREIGN AUTHORITY MAINTAINS ITSELF

The Sovereign, having no force other than the legislative power, acts only by means of the laws; and the laws being solely the authentic acts of the general will, the Sovereign cannot act save when the people is assembled. The people in assembly, I shall be told, is a mere chimera. It is so to-day, but two thousand years ago it was not so. Has man's nature changed?

The bounds of possibility, in moral matters, are less narrow than we imagine: it is our weaknesses, our vices and our prejudices that confine them. Base souls have no belief in great men; vile slaves smile in mockery at the name of liberty.

Let us judge of what can be done by what has been done. I shall say nothing of the Republics of ancient Greece; but the Roman Republic was, to my mind, a great State, and the town of Rome a great town. The last census showed that there were in Rome four hundred thousand citizens capable of bearing arms, and the last computation of the population of the Empire showed over four million citizens, excluding subjects, foreigners, women, children and slaves.

What difficulties might not be supposed to stand in the way of the frequent assemblage of the vast population of this capital and its neighbourhood. Yet few weeks passed without the Roman people being in assembly, and even being so several times. It exercised not only the rights of Sovereignty, but also a part of those of government. It dealt with certain matters, and judged certain cases, and this whole people was found in the public meeting-place hardly less often as magistrates than as citizens.

If we went back to the earliest history of nations, we should find that most ancient governments, even those of monarchical form, such as the Macedonian and the Frankish, had similar councils. In any case, the one incontestable fact I have given is an answer to all difficulties; it is good logic to reason from the actual to the possible.

CHAPTER XIII: THE SAME *(continued)*

It is not enough for the assembled people to have once fixed the constitution of the State by giving its sanction to a body of law; it is not enough for it to have set up a perpetual government, or provided once for all for the election of magistrates. Besides the extraordinary assemblies unforeseen circumstances may demand, there must be fixed periodical assemblies which cannot be abrogated or prorogued, so that on the proper day the people is legitimately called together by law, without need of any formal summoning.

But, apart from these assemblies authorised by their date alone, every assembly of the people not summoned by the magistrates appointed for that purpose, and in accordance with the prescribed forms, should be regarded as unlawful, and all its acts as null and void, because the command to assemble should itself proceed from the law.

The greater or less frequency with which lawful assemblies should occur depends on so many considerations that no exact rules about them can be given. It can only be said generally that the stronger the government the more often should the Sovereign show itself.

This, I shall be told, may do for a single town; but what is to be done when the State includes several? Is the sovereign authority to be divided? Or is it to be concentrated in a single town to which all the rest are made subject?

Neither the one nor the other, I reply. First, the sovereign authority is one and simple, and cannot be divided without being destroyed. In me second place, one town cannot, any more than one nation, legitimately be made subject to another, because the essence of the body politic lies in the reconciliation of obedience and liberty, and the words subject and Sovereign are identical correlatives the idea of which meets in the single word "citizen."

I answer further that the union of several towns in a single city is always bad, and that, if we wish to make such a union, we should not expect to avoid its natural disadvantages. It is useless to bring up abuses that belong to great States against one who desires to see only small ones; but how can small States be given the strength to resist great ones, as formerly the Greek towns resisted the Great King, and more recently Holland and Switzerland have resisted the House of Austria?

Nevertheless, if the State cannot be reduced to the right limits, there remains still one resource; this is, to allow no capital, to make the seat of government move from town to town, and to assemble by turn in each the Provincial Estates of the country.

People the territory evenly, extend everywhere the same rights, bear to every place in it abundance and life: by these means will the State become at once as strong and as well governed as possible. Remember that the walls of towns are built of the ruins of the houses of the countryside. For every palace I see raised in the capital, my mind's eye sees a whole country made desolate.

CHAPTER XIV: THE SAME *(continued)*

The moment the people is legitimately assembled as a sovereign body, the jurisdiction of the government wholly lapses, the executive power is suspended, and the person of the meanest citizen is as sacred and inviolable as that of the first magistrate; for in the presence of the person represented, representatives no longer exist. Most of the tumults that arose in the comitia at Rome were due to ignorance or neglect of this rule. The consuls were in them merely the presidents of the people; the tribunes were mere speakers;[12] the senate was nothing at all.

These intervals of suspension, during which the prince recognises or ought to recognise an actual superior, have always been viewed by him with alarm; and these assemblies of the people, which are the aegis of the body politic and the curb on die government, have at all times been the horror of rulers: who therefore never spare pains, objections, difficulties, and promises, to stop the citizens from having them. When the citizens are greedy, cowardly, and pusillanimous, and love ease more than liberty, they do not long hold out against the redoubled efforts of the government; and thus, as the resisting force incessantly grows, the sovereign authority ends by disappearing, and most cities fall and perish before their time.

But between the sovereign authority and arbitrary government there sometimes intervenes a mean power of which something must be said.

CHAPTER XV: DEPUTIES OR REPRESENTATIVES

As soon as public service ceases to be the chief business of the citizens, and they would rather serve with their money than with their persons, the State is not far from its fall. When it is necessary to march out to war, they pay troops and stay at home: when it is necessary to meet in council, they name deputies and stay at home. By reason of idleness and money, they end by having soldiers to enslave their country and representatives to sell it.

It is through the hustle of commerce and the arts, through the greedy self-interest of profit, and through softness and love of amenities that personal services are replaced by money payments. Men surrender a part of their profits in order to have time to increase them at leisure. Make gifts of money, and you will not be long without chains. The word *finance* is a slavish word, unknown in the city-state. In a country that is truly free, the citizens do everything with their own arms and nothing by means of money; so far from paying to be exempted from their duties, they would even pay for the privilege of fulfilling them themselves. I am far from taking the common view: I hold enforced labour to be less opposed to liberty than taxes.

The better the constitution of a State is, the more do public affairs encroach on private in the minds of the citizens. Private affairs are even of much less importance, because the aggregate of the common happiness furnishes a greater proportion of that of each individual, so that there is less for him to seek in particular cares. In a well-ordered city every man flies to the assemblies: under a bad government no one cares to stir a step to get to them, because no one is interested in what happens there, because it is foreseen that the general will will not prevail, and lastly because domestic cares are all-absorbing. Good laws lead to the making of better ones; bad ones bring about worse. As soon as any man says of the affairs of the State *What does it matter to me?* the State may be given up for lost.

---

[12] In nearly the same sense as this word has in the English Parliament. The similarity of these functions would have brought the consuls and the tribunes into conflict, even had all jurisdiction been suspended.

The lukewarmness of patriotism, the activity of private interest, the vastness of States, conquest and the abuse of government suggested the method of having deputies or representatives of the people in the national assemblies. These are what, in some countries, men have presumed to call the Third Estate. Thus the individual interest of two orders is put first and second; the public interest occupies only the third place.

Sovereignty, for the same reason as makes it inalienable, cannot be represented; it lies essentially in the general will, and will does not admit of representation: it is either the same, or other; there is no intermediate possibility. The deputies of the people, therefore, are not and cannot be its representatives: they are merely its stewards, and can carry through no definitive acts. Every law the people has not ratified in person is null and void—is, in fact, not a law. The people of England regards itself as free; but it is grossly mistaken; it is free only during the election of members of parliament. As soon as they are elected, slavery overtakes it, and it is nothing. The use it makes of the short moments of liberty it enjoys shows indeed that it deserves to lose them.

The idea of representation is modern; it comes to us from feudal government, from that iniquitous and absurd system which degrades humanity and dishonours the name of man. In ancient republics and even in monarchies, the people never had representatives; the word itself was unknown. It is very singular that in Rome, where the tribunes were so sacrosanct, it was never even imagined that they could usurp the functions of the people, and that in the midst of so great a multitude they never attempted to pass on their own authority a single plebiscitum. We can, however, form an idea of the difficulties caused sometimes by the people being so numerous, from what happened in the time of the Gracchi, when some of the citizens had to cast their votes from the roofs of buildings.

Where right and liberty are everything, disadvantages count for nothing. Among this wise people everything was given its just value, its lictors were allowed to do what its tribunes would never have dared to attempt; for it had no fear that its lictors would try to represent it.

To explain, however, in what way the tribunes did sometimes represent it, it is enough to conceive how the government represents the Sovereign. Law being purely the declaration of the general will, it is clear that, in the exercise of the legislative power, the people cannot be represented; but in that of the executive power, which is only the force that is applied to give the law effect, it both can and should be represented. We thus see that if we looked closely into the matter we should find that very few nations have any laws. However that may be, it is certain that the tribunes, possessing no executive power, could never represent the Roman people by right of the powers entrusted to them, but only by usurping those of the senate.

In Greece, all that the people had to do, it did for itself; it was constantly assembled in the public square. The Greeks lived in a mild climate; they had no natural greed; slaves did their work for them; their great concern was with liberty. Lacking the same advantages, how can you preserve the same rights? Your severer climates add to your needs;[13] for half the year your public squares are uninhabitable; the flatness of your languages unfits them for being heard in the open air; you sacrifice more for profit than for liberty, and fear slavery less than poverty.

What then? Is liberty maintained only by the help of slavery? It may be so. Extremes meet. Everything that is not in the course of nature has its disadvantages, civil society most of all. There are some unhappy circumstances in which we can only keep our liberty at others' expense, and where the citizen can be perfectly free only when the slave is most

---

[13] To adopt in cold countries the luxury and effeminacy of the East is to desire to submit to its chains; it is indeed to bow to them far more inevitably in our case than in theirs.

a slave. Such was the case with Sparta. As for you, modern peoples, you have no slaves, but you are slaves yourselves; you pay for their liberty with your own. It is in vain that you boast of this preference; I find in it more cowardice than humanity.

I do not mean by all this that it is necessary to have slaves, or that the right of slavery is legitimate: I am merely giving the reasons why modern peoples, believing themselves to be free, have representatives, while ancient peoples had none. In any case, the moment a people allows itself to be represented, it is no longer free: it no longer exists.

All things considered, I do not see that it is possible henceforth for the Sovereign to preserve among us the exercise of its rights, unless the city is very small. But if it is very small, it will be conquered? No. I will show later on how the external strength of a great people[14] may be combined with the convenient polity and good order of a small State.

CHAPTER XVI: THAT THE INSTITUTION OF GOVERNMENT IS NOT A CONTRACT

The legislative power once well established, the next thing is to establish similarly the executive power; for this latter, which operates only by particular acts, not being of the essence of the former, is naturally separate from it. Were it possible for the Sovereign, as such, to possess the executive power, right and fact would be so confounded that no one could tell what was law and what was not; and the body politic, thus disfigured, would soon fall a prey to the violence it was instituted to prevent.

As the citizens, by the social contract, are all equal, all can prescribe what all should do, but no one has a right to demand that another shall do what he does not do himself. It is strictly this right, which is indispensable for giving the body politic life and movement, that the Sovereign, in instituting the government, confers upon the prince.

It has been held that this act of establishment was a contract between the people and the rulers it sets over itself.—a contract in which conditions were laid down between the two parties binding the one to command and the other to obey. It will be admitted, I am sure, that this is an odd kind of contract to enter into. But let us see if this view can be upheld.

First, the supreme authority can no more be modified than it can be alienated; to limit it is to destroy it. It is absurd and contradictory for the Sovereign to set a superior over itself; to bind itself to obey a master would be to return to absolute liberty.

Moreover, it is clear that this contract between the people and such and such persons would be a particular act; and from this it follows that it can be neither a law nor an act of Sovereignty, and that consequently it would be illegitimate.

It is plain too that the contracting parties in relation to each other would be under the law of nature alone and wholly without guarantees of their mutual undertakings, a position wholly at variance with the civil state. He who has force at his command being always in a position to control execution, it would come to the same thing if the name "contract" were given to the act of one man who said to another; "I give you all my goods, on condition that you give me back as much of them as you please."

There is only one contract in the State, and that is the act of association, which in itself excludes the existence of a second. It is impossible to conceive of any public contract that would not be a violation of the first.

---

[14] I had intended to do this in the sequel to this work, when in dealing with external relations I came to the subject of confederations. The subject is quite new, and its principles have still to be laid down.

CHAPTER XVII: THE INSTITUTION OF GOVERNMENT

Under what general idea then should the act by which government is instituted be conceived as falling? I will begin by stating that the act is complex, as being composed of two others—the establishment' of the law and its execution.

By the former, the Sovereign decrees that there shall be a governing body established in this or that form; this act is clearly a law.

By the latter, the people nominates the rulers who are to be entrusted with the government that has been established. This nomination, being a particular act, is clearly not a second law, but merely a consequence of the first and a function of government.

The difficulty is to understand how there can be a governmental act before government exists, and how the people, which is only Sovereign or subject, can, under certain circumstances, become a prince or magistrate.

It is at this point that there is revealed one of the astonishing properties of the body politic, by means of which it reconciles apparently contradictory operations; for this is accomplished by a sudden conversion of Sovereignty into democracy, so that, without sensible change, and merely by virtue of a new relation of all to all, the citizens become magistrates and pass from general to particular acts, from legislation to the execution of the law.

This changed relation is no speculative subtlety without instances in practice: it happens every day in the English Parliament, where, on certain occasions, the Lower House resolves itself into Grand Committee, for the better discussion of affairs, and thus, from being at one moment a sovereign court, becomes at the next a mere commission; so that subsequently it reports to itself, as House of Commons, the result of its proceedings in Grand Committee, and debates over again under one name what it has already settled under another.

It is, indeed, the peculiar advantage of democratic government that it can be established in actuality by a simple act of the general will. Subsequently, this provisional government remains in power, if this form is adopted, or else establishes in the name of the Sovereign the government that is prescribed by law; and thus the whole proceeding is regular. It is impossible to set up government in any other manner legitimately and in accordance with the principles so far laid down.

CHAPTER XVIII: HOW TO CHECK THE USURPATIONS OF GOVERNMENT

What we have just said confirms Chapter XVI, and makes it clear that the institution of government is not a contract, but a law; that the depositaries of the executive power are not the people's masters, but its officers; that it can set them up and pull them down when it likes; that for them there is no question of contract, but of obedience; and that in taking charge of the functions the State imposes on them they are doing no more than fulfilling their duty as citizens, without having the remotest right to argue about the conditions.

When therefore the people sets up an hereditary government, whether it be monarchical and confined to one family, or aristocratic and confined to a class, what it enters into is not an undertaking; the administration is given a provisional form, until the people chooses to order it otherwise.

It is true that such changes are always dangerous, and that the established government should never be touched except when it comes to be incompatible with the public good; but the circumspection this involves is a maxim of policy and not a rule of right, and the State is no more bound to leave civil authority in the hands of its rulers than military authority in the hands of its generals.

It is also true that it is impossible to be too careful to observe, in such cases, all the formalities necessary to distinguish a regular and legitimate act from a seditious tumult, and the will of a whole people from the clamour of a faction. Here above all no further concession should be made to the untoward possibility than cannot, in the strictest logic, be refused it. From this obligation the prince derives a great advantage in preserving his power despite the people, without it being possible to say he has usurped it; for, seeming to avail himself only of his rights, he finds it very easy to extend them, and to prevent, under the pretext of keeping the peace, assemblies that are destined to the re-establishment of order; with the result that he takes advantage of a silence he does not allow to be broken, or of irregularities he causes to be committed, to assume that he has the support of those whom fear prevents from speaking, and to punish those who dare to speak. Thus it was that the decemvirs, first elected for one year and then kept on in office for a second, tried to perpetuate their power by forbidding the comitia to assemble; and by this easy method every government in the world, once clothed with the public power, sooner or later usurps the sovereign authority.

The periodical assemblies of which I have already spoken are designed to prevent or postpone this calamity, above all when they need no formal summoning; for in that case, the prince cannot stop them without openly declaring himself a law-breaker and an enemy of the State.

The opening of these assemblies, whose sole object is the maintenance of the social treaty, should always take the form of putting two propositions that may not be suppressed, which should be voted on separately.

The first is: "Does it please the Sovereign to preserve the present form of government?"

The second is: "Does it please the people to leave its administration in the hands of those who are actually in charge of it?"

I am here assuming what I think I have shown; that there is in the State no fundamental law that cannot be revoked, not excluding the social compact itself; for if all the citizens assembled of one accord to break the compact, it is impossible to doubt that it would be very legitimately broken. Grotius even thinks that each man can renounce his membership of his own State, and recover his natural liberty and his goods on leaving the country.[15] It would be indeed absurd if all the citizens in assembly could not do what each can do by himself.

---

[15] Provided, of course, he does not leave to escape his obligations and avoid having to serve his country in the hour of need. Flight in such a case would be criminal and punishable, and would be, not withdrawal, but desertion.

BOOK IV

CHAPTER I: THAT THE GENERAL WILL IS INDESTRUCTIBLE

As long as several men in assembly regard themselves as a single body, they have only a single will which is concerned with their common preservation and general well-being. In this case, all the springs of the State are vigorous and simple and its rules clear and luminous; there are no embroilments or conflicts of interests; the common good is everywhere clearly apparent, and only good sense is needed to perceive it. Peace, unity and equality are the enemies of political subtleties. Men who are upright and simple are difficult to deceive because of their simplicity; lures and ingenious pretexts fail to impose upon them, and they are not even subtle enough to be dupes. When, among the happiest people in the world, bands of peasants are seen regulating affairs of State under an oak, and always acting wisely, can we help scorning the ingenious methods of other nations, which make themselves illustrious and wretched with so much art and mystery?

A State so governed needs very few laws; and, as it becomes necessary to issue new ones, the necessity is universally seen. The first man to propose them merely says what all have already felt, and there is no question of factions or intrigues or eloquence in order to secure the passage into law of what every one has already decided to do, as soon as he is sure that the rest will act with him.

Theorists are led into error because, seeing only States that have been from the beginning wrongly constituted, they are struck by the impossibility of applying such a policy to them. They make great game of all the absurdities a clever rascal or an insinuating speaker might get the people of Paris or London to believe. They do not know that Cromwell would have been put to "the bells" by the people of Berne, and the Due de Beaufort on the treadmill by the Genevese.

But when the social bond begins to be relaxed and the State to grow weak, when particular interests begin to make themselves felt and the smaller societies to exercise an influence over the larger, the common interest changes and finds opponents: opinion is no longer unanimous; the general will ceases to be the will of all; contradictory views and debates arise; and the best advice is not taken without question.

Finally, when the State, on the eve of ruin, maintains only a vain, illusory and formal existence, when in every heart the social bond is broken, and the meanest interest brazenly lays hold of the sacred name of "public good," the general will becomes mute: all men, guided by secret motives, no more give their views as citizens than if the State had never been; and iniquitous decrees directed solely to private interest get passed under the name of laws.

Does it follow from this that the general will is exterminated or corrupted? Not at all: it is always constant, unalterable and pure; but it is subordinated to other wills which encroach upon its sphere. Each man, in detaching, his interest from the common interest, sees clearly that he cannot entirely separate them; but his share in the public mishaps seems to him negligible beside the exclusive good he aims at making his own. Apart from this particular good, he wills the general good in his own interest, as strongly as any one else. Even in selling his vote for money, he does not extinguish in himself the general will, but only eludes it. The fault he commits is that of changing the state of the question, and answering something different from what he is asked. Instead of saying, by his vote, "It is to the advantage of the State," he says, "It is of advantage to this or that man or party that this or that view should prevail." Thus the law of public order in assemblies is not so much to maintain in them the general will as to secure that the question be always put to it, and the answer always given by it.

I could here set down many reflections on the simple right of voting in every act of Sovereignty—a right which no-one can take from the citizens—and also on the right of stating views, making proposals, dividing and discussing, which the government is always most careful to leave solely to its members; but this important subject would need a treatise to itself, and it is impossible to say everything in a single work.

CHAPTER II: VOTING

It may be seen, from the last chapter, that the way in which general business is managed may give a clear enough indication of the actual state of morals and the health of the body politic. The more concert reigns in the assemblies, that is, the nearer opinion approaches unanimity, the greater is the dominance of the general will. On the other hand, long debates, dissensions and tumult proclaim the ascendancy of particular interests and the decline of the State.

This seems less clear when two or more orders enter into the constitution, as patricians and plebeians did at Rome; for quarrels between these two orders often disturbed the comitia, even in the best days of the Republic. But the exception is rather apparent than real; for then, through the defect that is inherent in the body politic, there were, so to speak, two States in one, and what is not true of the two together is true of either separately. Indeed, even in the most stormy times, the plebiscita of the people, when the Senate did not interfere with them, always went through quietly and by large majorities. The citizens having but one interest, the people had but a single will.

At the other extremity of the circle, unanimity recurs; this is the case when the citizens, having fallen into servitude, have lost both liberty and will. Fear and flattery then change votes into acclamation; deliberation ceases, and only worship or malediction is left. Such was the vile manner in which the senate expressed its views under the Emperors. It did so sometimes with absurd precautions. Tacitus observes that, under Otho, the senators, while they heaped curses on Vitellius, contrived at the same time to make a deafening noise, in order that, should he ever become their master, he might not know what each of them had said.

On these various considerations depend the rules by which the methods of counting votes and comparing opinions should be regulated, according as the general will is more or less easy to discover, and the State more or less in its decline.

There is but one law which, from its nature, needs unanimous consent. This is the social compact; for civil association is the most voluntary of all acts. Every man being born free and his own master, no-one, under any pretext whatsoever, can make any man subject without his consent. To decide that the son of a slave is born a slave is to decide that he is not born a man.

If then there are opponents when the social compact is made, their opposition does not invalidate the contract, but merely prevents them from being included in it. They are foreigners among citizens. When the State is instituted, residence constitutes consent; to dwell within its territory is to submit to the Sovereign.[1]

---

[1] This should of course be understood as applying to a free State; for elsewhere family, goods, lack of a refuge, necessity, or violence may detain a man in a country against his will; and then his dwelling there no longer by itself implies his consent to the contract or to its violation.

Apart from this primitive contract, the vote of the majority always binds all the rest. This follows from the contract itself. But it is asked how a man can be both free and forced to conform to wills that are not his own. How are the opponents at once free and subject to laws they have not agreed to?

I retort that the question is wrongly put. The citizen gives his consent to all the laws, including those which are passed in spite of his opposition, and even those which punish him when he dares to break any of them. The constant will of all the members of the State is the general will; by virtue of it they are citizens and free.[2] When in the popular assembly a law is proposed, what the people is asked is not exactly whether it approves or rejects the proposal, but whether it is in conformity with the general will, which is their will. Each man, in giving his vote, states his opinion on that point; and the general will is found by counting votes. When therefore the opinion that is contrary to my own prevails, this proves neither more nor less than that I was mistaken, and that what I thought to be the general will was not so. If my particular opinion had carried the day I should have achieved the opposite of what was my will and it is in that case that I should not have been free.

This presupposes, indeed, that all the qualities of the general will still reside in the majority: when they cease to do so, whatever side a man may take, liberty is no longer possible.

In my earlier demonstration of how particular wills are substituted for the general will in public deliberation, I have adequately pointed out the practicable methods of avoiding this abuse; and I shall have more to say of them later on. I have also given the principles for determining the proportional number of votes for declaring that will. A difference of one vote destroys equality; a single opponent destroys unanimity; but between equality and unanimity, there are several grades of unequal division, at each of which this proportion may be fixed in accordance with the condition and the needs of the body politic.

There are two general rules that may serve to regulate this relation. First, the more grave and important the questions discussed, the nearer should the opinion that is to prevail approach unanimity. Secondly, the more the matter in hand calls for speed, the smaller the prescribed difference in the numbers of votes may be allowed to become: where an instant decision has to be reached, a majority of one vote should be enough. The first of these two rules seems more in harmony with the laws, and the second with practical affairs. In any case, it is the combination of them that gives the best proportions for determining the majority necessary.

CHAPTER III: ELECTIONS

In the elections of the prince and the magistrates, which are, as I have said, complex acts, there are two possible methods of procedure, choice and lot. Both have been employed in various republics, and a highly complicated mixture of the two still survives in the election of the Doge at Venice.

"Election by lot," says Montesquieu, "is democratic in nature." I agree that it is so; but in what sense? "The lot," he goes on, "is a way of making choice that is unfair to

---

[2] At Genoa, the word *Liberty* may be read over the front of the prisons and on the chains of the galley-slaves. This application of the device is good and just It is indeed only malefactors of all estates who prevent the citizen from being free. In the country in which all such men were in the galleys, the most perfect liberty would be enjoyed.

nobody; it leaves each citizen a reasonable hope of serving his country." These are not reasons.

If we bear in mind that the election of rulers is a function of government, and not of Sovereignty, we shall see why the lot is the method more natural to democracy, in which the administration is better in proportion as the number of its acts is small.

In every real democracy, magistracy is not an advantage, but a burdensome charge which cannot justly be imposed on one individual rather than another. The law alone can lay the charge on him on whom the lot falls. For, the conditions being then the same for all, and the choice not depending on any human will, there is no particular application to alter the universality of the law.

In an aristocracy, the prince chooses the prince, the government is preserved by itself, and voting is rightly ordered.

The instance of the election of the Doge of Venice confirms, instead of destroying, this distinction; the mixed form suits a mixed government. For it is an error to take the government of Venice for a real aristocracy. If the people has no share in the government, the nobility is itself the people. A host of poor Barnabotes never gets near any magistracy, and its nobility consists merely in the empty title of Excellency, and in the right to sit in the Great Council. As this Great Council is as numerous as our General Council at Geneva, its illustrious members have no more privileges than our plain citizens. It is indisputable that, apart from the extreme disparity between the two republics, the *bourgeoisie* of Geneva is exactly equivalent to the *patriciate* of Venice; our *natives* and *inhabitants* correspond to the *townsmen* and the *people* of Venice; our *peasants* correspond to the *subjects* on the mainland; and, however that republic be regarded, if its size be left out of account, its government is no more aristocratic than our own. The whole difference is that, having no life-ruler, we do not, like Venice, need to use the lot.

Election by lot would have few disadvantages in a real democracy, in which, as equality would everywhere exist in morals and talents as well as in principles and fortunes, it would become almost a matter of indifference who was chosen. But I have already said that a real democracy is only an ideal.

When choice and lot are combined, positions that require special talents, such as military posts, should be filled by the former; the latter does for cases, such as judicial offices, in which good sense, justice, and integrity are enough, because in a State that is well constituted, these qualities are common to all the citizens.

Neither lot nor vote has any place in monarchical government. The monarch being by right sole prince and only magistrate, the choice of his lieutenants belongs to none but him. When the Abbé de Saint-Pierre proposed that the Councils of the King of France should be multiplied, and their members elected by ballot, he did not see that he was proposing to change the form of government.

I should now speak of the methods of giving and counting opinions in the assembly of the people; but perhaps an account of this aspect of the Roman constitution will more forcibly illustrate all the rules I could lay down. It is worth the while of a judicious reader to follow in some detail the working of public and private affairs in a Council consisting of two hundred thousand men.

CHAPTER IV: THE ROMAN COMITIA

We are without well-certified records of the first period of Rome's existence; it even appears very probable that most of the stories told about it are fables; indeed, generally speaking, the most instructive part of the history of peoples, that which deals with their foundation, is what we have least of. Experience teaches us every day what causes lead to the revolutions of empires; but, as no new peoples are now formed, we have almost nothing beyond conjecture to go upon in explaining how they were created.

The customs we find established show at least that these customs had an origin. The traditions that go back to those origins, that have the greatest authorities behind them, and that are confirmed by the strongest proofs, should pass for the most certain. These are the rules I have tried to follow in inquiring how the freest and most powerful people on earth exercised its supreme power.

After the foundation of Rome, the new-born republic, that is, the army of its founder, composed of Albans, Sabines and foreigners, was divided into three classes, which, from this division, took the name of *tribes*. Each of these tribes was subdivided into ten *curiæ*, and each *curia* into *decuriæ*, headed by leaders called *curiones* and *decuriones*.

Besides this, out of each tribe was taken a body of one hundred *Equites* or Knights, called a *century*, which shows that these divisions, being unnecessary in a town, were at first merely military. But an instinct for greatness seems to have led the little township of Rome to provide itself in advance with a political system suitable for the capital of the world.

Out of this original division an awkward situation soon arose. The tribes of the Albans (Ramnenses) and the Sabines (Tatienses) remained always in the same condition, while that of the foreigners (Luceres) continually grew as more and more foreigners came to live at Rome, so that it soon surpassed the others in strength. Servius remedied this dangerous fault by changing the principle of cleavage, and substituting for the racial division, which he abolished, a new one based on the quarter of the town inhabited by each tribe. Instead of three tribes he created four, each occupying and named after one of the hills of Rome. Thus, while redressing the inequality of the moment, he also provided for the future; and in order that the division might be one of persons as well as localities, he forbade the inhabitants of one quarter to migrate to another, and so prevented the mingling of the races.

He also doubled the three old centuries of Knights and added twelve more, still keeping the old names, and by this simple and prudent method, succeeded in making a distinction between the body of Knights and the people, without a murmur from the latter.

To the four urban tribes Servius added fifteen others called rural tribes, because they consisted of those who lived in the country, divided into fifteen cantons. Subsequently, fifteen more were created, and the Roman people finally found itself divided into thirty-five tribes, as it remained down to the end of the Republic.

The distinction between urban and rural tribes had one effect which is worth mention, both because it is without parallel elsewhere, and because to it Rome owed the preservation of her morality and the enlargement of her empire. We should have expected that the urban tribes would soon monopolise power and honours, and lose no time in bringing the rural tribes into disrepute; but what happened was exactly the reverse. The taste of the early Romans for country life is well known. This taste they owed to their wise founder, who made rural and military labours go along with liberty, and, so to speak, relegated to the town arts, crafts, intrigue, fortune and slavery.

Since therefore all Rome's most illustrious citizens lived in the fields and tilled the earth, men grew used to seeking there alone the mainstays of the republic. This condition, being that of the best patricians, was honoured by all men; the simple and laborious life of the villager was preferred to the slothful and idle life of the *bourgeoisie* of Rome; and he who, in the town, would have been but a wretched proletarian, became, as a labourer in the fields, a respected citizen. Not without reason, says Varro, did our great-souled ancestors establish in the village the nursery of the sturdy and valiant men who defended them in time of war and provided for their Sustenance in time of peace. Pliny states positively that the country tribes were honoured because of the men of whom they were composed; while cowards men wished to dishonour were transferred, as a public disgrace, to the town tribes. The Sabine Appius Claudius, when he had come to settle in Rome, was loaded with honours and enrolled in a rural tribe, which subsequently took his family name. Lastly, freedmen always entered the urban, and never the rural, tribes: nor is there a single example, throughout the Republic, of a freedman, though he had become a citizen, reaching any magistracy.

This was an excellent rule; but it was carried so far that in the end it led to a change and certainly to an abuse in the political system.

First the censors, after having for a long time claimed the right of transferring citizens arbitrarily from one tribe to another, allowed most persons to enroll themselves in whatever tribe they pleased. This permission certainly did no good, and further robbed the censorship of one of its greatest resources. Moreover, as the great and powerful all got themselves enrolled in the country tribes, while the freedmen who had become citizens remained with the populace in the town tribes, both soon ceased to have any local or territorial meaning, and all were so confused that the members of one could not be told from those of another except by the registers; so that the idea of the word *tribe* became personal instead of real, or rather came to be little more than a chimera.

It happened in addition that the town tribes, being more on the spot, were often the stronger in the comitia and sold the State to those who stooped to buy the votes of the rabble composing them.

As the founder had set up ten *curiæ* in each tribe, the whole Roman people, which was then contained within the walls, consisted of thirty *curia*, each with its temples, its gods, its officers, its priests and its festivals, which were called *compitalia* and corresponded to the *paganalia,* held in later times by the rural tribes.

When Servius made his new division, as the thirty *curiæ* could not be shared equally between his four tribes, and as he was unwilling to interfere with them, they became a further division of the inhabitants of Rome, quite independent of the tribes: but in the case of the rural tribes and their members there was no question of *cutiæ* as the tribes had then become a purely civil institution, and, a new system of levying troops having been introduced, the military divisions of Romulus were superfluous. Thus, although every citizen was enrolled in a tribe, there were very many who were not members of a *curia*.

Servius made yet a third division, quite distinct from the two we have mentioned, which became, in its effects, the most important of all. He distributed the whole Roman people into six classes, distinguished neither by place nor by person, but by wealth; the first classes included the rich, the last the poor, and those between persons of moderate means. These six classes were subdivided into one hundred and ninety-three other bodies, called centuries, which were so divided that the first class alone comprised more than half of them, while the last comprised only one. Thus the class that had the smallest number of members had the largest number of centuries, and the whole of the last class only counted as a single subdivision, although it alone included more than half the inhabitants of Rome.

In order that the people might have the less insight into the results of this arrangement, Servius tried to give it a military tone: in the second class he inserted two centuries of armourers, and in the fourth two of makers of instruments of war: in each class, except the last, he distinguished young and old, that is, those who were under an obligation to bear arms and those whose age gave them legal exemption. It was this distinction, rather than that of wealth, which required frequent repetition of the census or counting. Lastly, he ordered that the assembly should be held in the Campus Martius, and that all who were of age to serve should come there armed.

The reason for his not making in the last class also the division of young and old was that the populace, of whom it was composed, was not given the right to bear arms for its country: a man had to possess a hearth to acquire the right to defend it, and of all the troops of beggars who to-day lend lustre to the armies of kings, there is perhaps not one who would not have been driven with scorn out of a Roman cohort, at a time when soldiers were the defenders of liberty.

In this last class, however, *proletarians* were distinguished from *capite censi* The former, not quite reduced to nothing, at least gave the State citizens, and sometimes, when the need was pressing, even soldiers. Those who had nothing at all, and could be numbered only by counting heads, were regarded as of absolutely no account, and Marius was the first who stooped to enroll them.

Without deciding now whether this third arrangement was good or bad in itself, I think I may assert that it could have been made practicable only by the simple morals, the disinterestedness, the liking for agriculture and the scorn for commerce and for love of gain which characterised the early Romans. Where is the modern people among whom consuming greed, unrest, intrigue, continual removals, and perpetual changes of fortune, could let such a system last for twenty years without turning the State upside down? We must indeed observe that morality and the censorship, being stronger than this institution, corrected its defects at Rome, and that the rich man found himself degraded to the class of the poor for making too much display of his riches.

From all this it is easy to understand why only five classes are almost always mentioned, though there were really six. The sixth, as it furnished neither soldiers to the army nor votes in the Campus Martius,[3] and was almost without function in the State, was seldom regarded as of any account.

These were the various ways in which the Roman people was divided. Let us now see the effect on the assemblies. When lawfully summoned, these were called *comitia*: they were usually held in the public square at Rome or in the Campus Martius, and were distinguished as *Comitia Curiata, Comitia Centuriata,* and *Comitia Tributa,* according to the form under which they were convoked. The *Comitia Curiata* were founded by Romulus; the *Centuriata* by Servius; and the *Tributa* by the tribunes of the people. No law received its sanction and no magistrate was elected, save in the comitia; and as every citizen was enrolled in a *curia,* a century, or a tribe, it follows that no citizen was excluded from the right of voting, and that the Roman people was truly sovereign both *de jure* and *de facto.*

For the comitia to be lawfully assembled, and for their acts to have the force of law, three conditions were necessary. First, the body or magistrate convoking them had to possess the necessary authority; secondly, the assembly had to be held on a day allowed by law; and thirdly, the auguries had to be favourable.

The reason for the first regulation needs no explanation; the second is a matter of policy. Thus, the comitia might not be held on festivals or market-days, when the country-folk, coming to Rome on business, had not time to spend the day in the public square. By means of the third, the senate held in check the proud and restive people, and meekly restrained the ardour of seditious tribunes, who, however, found more than one way of escaping this hindrance.

---

[3] I say "in the Campus Martius" because it was there that the comitia assembled by centuries; in its two other forms the people assembled in the *forum* or elsewhere; and then the *capite censi* had as much influence and authority as the foremost citizens.

Laws and the election of rulers were not the only questions submitted to the judgment of the comitia: as the Roman people had taken on itself the most important functions of government, it may be said that the lot of Europe was regulated in its assemblies. The variety of their objects gave rise to the various forms these took, according to the matters on which they had to pronounce.

In order to judge of these various forms, it is enough to compare them. Romulus, when he set up *curiæ*, had in view the checking of the senate by the people, and of the people by the senate, while maintaining his ascendancy over both alike. He therefore gave the people, by means of this assembly, all the authority of numbers to balance that of power and riches, which he left to the patricians. But, after the spirit of monarchy, he left all the same a greater advantage to the patricians in the influence of their clients on the majority of votes. This excellent institution of patron and client was a masterpiece of statesmanship and humanity without which the patriciate, being flagrantly in contradiction to the republican spirit, could not have survived. Rome alone has the honour of having given to the world this great example, which never led to any abuse, and yet has never been followed.

As the assemblies by *curiæ* persisted under the kings till the time of Servius, and the reign of the later Tarquin was not regarded as legitimate, royal laws were called generally *leges curiatæ*.

Under the Republic, the *curiæ* still confined to the four urban tribes, and including only the populace of Rome, suited neither the senate, which led the patricians, nor the tribunes, who, though plebeians, were at the head of the well-to-do citizens. They therefore fell into disrepute, and their degradation was such, that thirty lictors used to assemble and do what the *Comitia Curiata* should have done.

The division by centuries was so favourable to the aristocracy that it is hard to see at first how the senate ever failed to carry the day in the comitia bearing their name, by which the consuls, the censors and the other curule magistrates were elected. Indeed, of the hundred and ninety-three centuries into which the six classes of the whole Roman people were divided, the first class contained ninety-eight; and, as voting went solely by centuries, this class alone had a majority over all the rest. When all these centuries were in agreement, the rest of the votes were not even taken; the decision of the smallest number passed for that of the multitude, and it may be said that, in the *Comitia Centuriata*, decisions were regulated far more by depth of purses than by the number of votes.

But this extreme authority was modified in two ways. First, the tribunes as a rule, and always a great number of plebeians, belonged to the class of the rich, and so counterbalanced the influence of the patricians in the first class.

The second way was this. Instead of causing the centuries to vote throughout in order, which would have meant beginning always with the first, the Romans always chose one by lot which proceeded alone to the election; after this all the centuries were summoned another day according to their rank, and the same election was repeated, and as a rule confirmed. Thus the authority of example was taken away from rank, and given to the lot on a democratic principle.

From this custom resulted a further advantage. The citizens from the country had time, between the two elections, to inform themselves of the merits of the candidate who had been provisionally nominated, and did not have to vote without knowledge of the case. But, under the pretext of hastening matters, the abolition of this custom was achieved, and both elections were held on the same day.

The *Comitia Tributa* were properly the council of the Roman people. They were convoked by the tribunes alone; at them the tribunes were elected and passed their plebiscita. The senate not only had no standing in them, but even no right to be present; and the senators, being forced to obey laws on which they could not vote, were in this respect less free than the meanest citizens. This injustice was altogether ill-conceived, and was alone enough to invalidate the decrees of a body to which all its members were not admitted. Had all the patricians attended the comitia by virtue of the right they had as citizens, they would not, as mere private individuals, have had any considerable influence on a vote reckoned by counting heads, where the meanest proletarian was as good as the *princeps senatus.*

It may be seen, therefore, that besides the order which was achieved by these various ways of distributing so great a people and taking its votes, the various methods were not reducible to forms indifferent in themselves, but the results of each were relative to the objects which caused it to be preferred.

Without going here into further details, we may gather from what has been said above that the *Comitia Tributa* were the most favourable to popular government, and the *Comitia Centuriata* to aristocracy. The *Comitia Curiata,* in which the populace of Rome formed the majority, being fitted only to further tyranny and evil designs, naturally fell into disrepute, and even seditious persons abstained from using a method which too clearly revealed their projects. It is indisputable that the whole majesty of the Roman people lay solely in the *Comitia Centuriata,* which alone included all; for the *Comitia Curiata* excluded the rural tribes, and the *Comitia Tributa* the senate and the patricians.

As for the method of taking the vote, it was among the ancient Romans as simple as their morals, although not so simple as at Sparta. Each man declared his vote aloud, and a clerk duly wrote it down; the majority in each tribe determined the vote of the tribe, the majority of the tribes that of the people, and so with *curiæ* and centuries. This custom was good as long as honesty was triumphant among the citizens, and each man was ashamed to vote publicly in favour of an unjust proposal or an unworthy subject; but, when the people grew corrupt and votes were bought, it was fitting that voting should be secret in order that purchasers might be restrained by mistrust, and rogues be given the means of not being traitors.

I know that Cicero attacks this change, and attributes partly to it the ruin of the Republic. But though I feel the weight Cicero's authority must carry on such a point, I cannot agree with him; I hold, on die contrary, that, for want of enough such changes, the destruction of the State must be hastened. Just as the regimen of health does riot suit the sick, we should not wish to govern a people that has been corrupted by the laws that a good people requires. There is no better proof of this rule than the long life of the Republic of Venice, of which the shadow still exists, solely because its laws are suitable only for men who are wicked.

The citizens were provided, therefore, with tablets by means of which each man could vote without any one knowing how he voted: new methods were also introduced for collecting the tablets, for counting voices, for comparing numbers, etc.; but all these precautions did not prevent the good faith of the officers charged with these functions[4] from being often suspect. Finally, to prevent intrigues and trafficking in votes, edicts were issued; but their very number proves how useless they were.

Towards the close of the Republic, it was often necessary to have recourse to extraordinary expedients in order to supplement the inadequacy of the laws. Sometimes miracles were supposed; but this method, while it might impose on the people, could not impose on those who governed. Sometimes an assembly was hastily called together, before the candidates had time to form their factions: sometimes a whole sitting was occupied with talk, when it was seen that the people had been won over and was on the

---

[4] Custodes, diribitores, rogatores suffragiorum.

point of taking up a wrong position. But in the end ambition eluded all attempts to check it; and the most incredible fact of all is that, in the midst of all these abuses, the vast people, thanks to its ancient regulations, never ceased to elect magistrates, to pass laws, to judge cases, and to carry through business both public and private, almost as easily as the senate itself could have done.

CHAPTER V: THE TRIBUNATE

When an exact proportion cannot be established between the constituent parts of the State, or when causes that cannot be removed continually alter the relation of one part to another, recourse is had to the institution of a peculiar magistracy that enters into no corporate unity with the rest. This restores to each term its right relation to the others, and provides a link or middle term between either prince and people, or prince and Sovereign, or, if necessary, both at once.

This body, which I shall call the *tribunate*, is the preserver of the laws and of the legislative power. It serves sometimes to protect the Sovereign against the government, as the tribunes of the people did at Rome; sometimes to uphold the government against the people, as the Council of Ten now does at Venice; and sometimes to maintain the balance between the two, as the Ephors did at Sparta.

The tribunate is not a constituent part of the city, and should have no share in either legislative or executive power; but this very fact makes its own power the greater: for, while it can do nothing, it can prevent anything from being done. It is more sacred and more revered, as the defender of the laws, than the prince who executes them, or than the Sovereign which ordains them. This was seen very clearly at Rome, when the proud patricians, for all their scorn of the people, were forced to bow before one of its officers, who had neither auspices nor jurisdiction.

The tribunate, wisely tempered, is the strongest support a good constitution can have; but if its strength is ever so little excessive, it upsets the whole State. Weakness, on the other hand, is not natural to it: provided it is something, it is never less than it should be.

It degenerates into tyranny when it usurps the executive power, which it should confine itself to restraining, and when it tries to dispense with the laws, which it should confine itself to protecting. The immense power of the Ephors, harmless as long as Sparta preserved its morality, hastened corruption when once it had begun. The blood of Agis, slaughtered by these tyrants, was avenged by his successor; the crime and the punishment of the Ephors alike hastened the destruction of the republic, and after Cleomenes Sparta ceased to be of any account. Rome perished in the same way: the excessive power of the tribunes, which they had usurped by degrees, finally served, with the help of laws made to secure liberty, as a safeguard for the emperors who destroyed it. As for the Venetian Council of Ten, it is a tribunal of blood, an object of horror to patricians and people alike; and, so far from giving a lofty protection to the laws, it does nothing, now they have become degraded, but strike in the darkness blows of which no one dare take note.

The tribunate, like the government, grows weak as the number of its members increases. When the tribunes of the Roman people, who first numbered only two, and then five, wished to double that number, the senate let them do so, in the confidence that it could use one to check another, as indeed it afterwards freely did.

The best method of preventing usurpations by so formidable a body, though no government has yet made use of it, would be not to make it permanent, but to regulate the periods during which it should remain in abeyance. These intervals, which should not be long enough to give abuses time to grow strong, may be so fixed by law that they can easily be shortened at need by extraordinary commissions.

This method seems to me to have no disadvantages, because, as I have said, the tribunate, which forms no part of the constitution, can be removed without the constitution being affected. It seems to be also efficacious, because a newly restored magistrate starts not with the power his predecessor exercised, but with that which the law allows him.

CHAPTER VI: THE DICTATORSHIP

The inflexibility of the laws, which prevents them from adapting themselves to circumstances, may, in certain cases, render them disastrous, and make them bring about, at a time of crisis, the ruin of the State. The order and slowness of the forms they enjoin require a space of time which circumstances sometimes withhold. A thousand cases against which the legislator has made no provision may present themselves, and it is a highly necessary part of foresight to be conscious that everything cannot be foreseen.

It is wrong therefore to wish to make political institutions so strong as to render it impossible to suspend their operation. Even Sparta allowed its laws to lapse.

However, none but the greatest dangers can counter-balance that of changing the public order, and the sacred power of the laws should never be arrested save when the existence of the country is at stake. In these rare and obvious cases, provision is made for the public security by a particular act entrusting it to him who is most worthy. This commitment may be carried out in either of two ways, according to the nature of the danger.

If increasing the activity of the government is a sufficient remedy, power is concentrated in the hands of one or two of its members: in this case the change is not in the authority of the laws, but only in the form of administering them. If, on the other hand, the peril is of such a kind that the paraphernalia of the laws are an obstacle to their preservation, the method is to nominate a supreme ruler, who shall silence all the laws and suspend for a moment the sovereign authority. In such a case, there is no doubt about the general will, and it is clear that the people's first intention is that the State shall not perish. Thus the suspension of the legislative authority is in no sense its abolition; the magistrate who silences it cannot make it speak; he dominates it, but cannot represent it. He can do anything, except make laws.

The first method was used by the Roman senate when, in a consecrated formula, it charged the consuls to provide for the safety of the Republic. The second was employed when one of the two consuls nominated a dictator:[5] a custom Rome borrowed from Alba.

During the first period of the Republic, recourse was very often had to the dictatorship, because the State had not yet a firm enough basis to be able to maintain itself by the strength of its constitution alone. As the state of morality then made superfluous many of the precautions which would have been necessary at other times, there was no fear that a dictator would abuse his authority, or try to keep it beyond his term of office. On the contrary, so much power appeared to be burdensome to him who was clothed with it, and he made all speed to lay it down, as if taking the place of the laws had been too troublesome and too perilous a position to retain.

It is therefore the danger not of its abuse, but of its cheapening, that makes me attack the indiscreet use of this supreme magistracy in the earliest times. For as long as it was freely employed at elections, dedications and purely formal functions, there was danger

---

[5] The nomination was made secretly by night, as if there were something shameful in setting a man above the laws.

of its becoming less formidable in time of need, and of men growing accustomed to regarding as empty a title that was used only on occasions of empty ceremonial.

Towards the end of the Republic, the Romans, having grown more circumspect, were as unreasonably sparing in the use of the dictatorship as they had formerly been lavish. It is easy to see that their fears were without foundation, that the weakness of the capital secured it against the magistrates who were in its midst; that a dictator might, in certain cases, defend the public liberty, but could never endanger it; and that the chains of Rome would be forged, not in Rome itself, but in her armies. The weak resistance offered by Marius to Sulla, and by Pompey to Cæsar, clearly showed what was to be expected from authority at home against force from abroad.

This misconception led the Romans to make great mistakes; such, for example, as the failure to nominate a dictator in the Catilinarian conspiracy. For, as only the city itself, with at most some province in Italy, was concerned, the unlimited authority the laws gave to the dictator would have enabled him to make short work of the conspiracy, which was, in fact, stifled only by a combination of lucky chances human prudence had no right to expect.

Instead, the senate contented itself with entrusting its whole power to the consuls, so that Cicero, in order to take effective action, was compelled on a capital point to exceed his powers; and if, in the first transports of joy, his conduct was approved, he was justly called, later on, to account for the blood of citizens spilt in violation of the laws. Such a reproach could never have been levelled at a dictator. But the consul's eloquence carried the day; and he himself, Roman though he was, loved his own glory better than his country, and sought, not so much the most lawful and secure means of saving the State, as to get for himself the whole honour of having done so.[6] He was therefore justly honoured as the liberator of Rome, and also justly punished as a law-breaker. However brilliant his recall may have been, it was undoubtedly an act of pardon.

However this important trust be conferred, it is important that its duration should be fixed at a very brief period, incapable of being ever prolonged. In the crises which lead to its adoption, the State is either soon lost, or soon saved; and, the present need passed, the dictatorship becomes either tyrannical or idle. At Rome, where dictators held office for six months only, most of them abdicated before their time was up. If their term had been longer, they might well have tried to prolong it still further, as the decemvirs did when chosen for a year. The dictator had only time to provide against the need that had caused him to be chosen; he had none to think of further projects.

CHAPTER VII: THE CENSORSHIP

As the law is the declaration of the general will, the censorship is the declaration of the public judgment: public opinion is the form of law which the censor administers, and, like the prince, only applies to particular cases.

The censorial tribunal, so far from being the arbiter of the people's opinion, only declares it, and, as soon as the two part company, its decisions are null and void.

It is useless to distinguish the morality of a nation from the objects of its esteem; both depend on the same principle and are necessarily indistinguishable. There is no people on earth the choice of whose pleasures is not decided by opinion rather than nature. Right men's opinions, and their morality will purge itself. Men always love what is good or what they find good; it is in judging what is good that they go wrong. This judgment,

---

[6] That is what he could not be sure of, if he proposed a dictator; for he dared not nominate himself, and could not be certain that his colleague would nominate him.

therefore, is what must be regulated. He who judges of morality judges of honour; and he who judges of honour finds his law in opinion.

The opinions of a people are derived from its constitution; although the law does not regulate morality, it is legislation that gives it birth. When legislation grows weak, morality degenerates; but in such cases the judgment of the censors will not do what the force of the laws has failed to effect.

From this it follows that the censorship may be useful for the preservation of morality, but can never be so for its restoration. Set up censors while the laws are vigorous; as soon as they have lost their vigour, all hope is gone; no legitimate power can retain force when the laws have lost it.

The censorship upholds morality by preventing opinion from growing corrupt, by preserving its rectitude by means of wise applications, and sometimes even by fixing it when it is still uncertain. The employment of seconds in duels, which had been carried to wild extremes in the kingdom of France, was done away with merely by these words in a royal edict: "As for those who are cowards enough to call upon seconds." This judgment, in anticipating that of the public, suddenly decided it. But when edicts from the same source tried to pronounce duelling itself an act of cowardice, as indeed it is, then, since common opinion does not regard it as such, the public took no notice of a decision on a point on which its mind was already made up.

I have stated elsewhere[7] that as public opinion is not subject to any constraint, there need be no trace of it in the tribunal set up to represent it. It is impossible to admire too much the art with which this resource, which we moderns have wholly lost, was employed by the Romans, and still more by the Lacedæmonians.

A man of bad morals having made a good proposal in the Spartan Council, the Ephors neglected it, and caused the same proposal to be made by a virtuous citizen. What an honour for the one, and what a disgrace for the other, without praise or blame of either! Certain drunkards from Samos[8] polluted the tribunal of the Ephors: the next day, a public edict gave Samians permission to be filthy. An actual punishment would not have been so severe as such an impunity. When Sparta has pronounced on what is or is not right, Greece makes no appeal from her judgments.

CHAPTER VIII: CIVIL RELIGION

At first men had no kings save the gods, and no government save theocracy. They reasoned like Caligula, and, at that period, reasoned aright. It takes a long time for feeling so to change that men can make up their minds to take their equals as masters, in the hope that they will profit by doing so.

From the mere fact that God was set over every political society, it followed that there were as many gods as peoples. Two peoples that were strangers the one to the other, and almost always enemies, could not long recognise the same master: two armies giving battle could not obey the same leader. National divisions thus led to polytheism, and this in turn gave rise to theological and civil intolerance, which, as we shall see hereafter, are by nature the same.

The fancy the Greeks had for rediscovering their gods among the barbarians arose from the way they had of regarding themselves as the natural Sovereigns of such peoples.

---

[7] I merely call attention in this chapter to a subject with which I have dealt at greater length in my *Letter to M. d'Alembert.*

[8] They were from another island, which the delicacy of our language forbids me to name on this occasion.

But there is nothing so absurd as the erudition which in our days identifies and confuses gods of different nations. As if Moloch, Saturn and Chronos could be the same god! As if the Phœnician Baal, the Greek Zeus, and the Latin Jupiter could be the same! As if there could still be anything common to imaginary beings with different names!

If it is asked how in pagan times, where each State had its cult and its gods, there were no wars of religion, I answer that it was precisely because each State, having its own cult as well as its own government, made no distinction between its gods and its laws. Political war was also theological; the provinces of the gods were, so to speak, fixed by the boundaries of nations. The god of one people had no right over another. The gods of the pagans were not jealous gods; they shared among themselves the empire of the world: even Moses and the Hebrews sometimes lent themselves to this view by speaking of the God of Israel. It is true, they regarded as powerless the gods of the Canaanites, a proscribed people condemned to destruction, whose place they were to take; but remember how they spoke of the divisions of the neighbouring peoples they were forbidden to attack! "Is not the possession of what belongs to your god Chamos lawfully your due?" said Jephthah to the Ammonites. "We have the same title to the lands our conquering God has made his own."[9] Here, I think, there is a recognition that the rights of Chamos and those of the God of Israel are of the same nature.

But when the Jews, being subject to the kings of Babylon, and, subsequently, to those of Syria, still obstinately refused to recognise any god save their own, their refusal was regarded as rebellion against their conqueror, and drew down on them the persecutions we read of in their history, which are without parallel till the coming of Christianity.[10]

Every religion, therefore, being attached solely to the laws of the State which prescribed it, there was no way of converting a people except by enslaving it, and there could be no missionaries save conquerors. The obligation to change cults being the law to which the vanquished yielded, it was necessary to be victorious before suggesting such a change. So far from men fighting for the gods, the gods, as in Homer, fought for men; each asked his god for victory, and repaid him with new altars. The Romans, before taking a city, summoned its gods to quit it; and, in leaving the Tarentines their outraged gods, they regarded them as subject to their own and compelled to do them homage. They left the vanquished their gods as they left them their laws. A wreath to the Jupiter of the Capitol was often the only tribute they imposed.

Finally, when, along with their empire, the Romans had spread their cult and their gods, and had themselves often adopted those of the vanquished, by granting to both alike the rights of the city, the peoples of that vast empire insensibly found themselves with multitudes of gods and cults, everywhere almost the same; and thus paganism throughout the known world finally came to be one and the same religion.

It was in these circumstances that Jesus came to set up on earth a spiritual kingdom, which, by separating the theological from the political system, made the State no longer one, and brought about the internal divisions which have never ceased to trouble

---

[9] Nonne ea quæ possidet Chamos deus tuus, tibi jure debentur? (Judges xi. 24). Such is the text in the Vulgate. Father de Carrières translates: "Do you not regard yourselves as having a right to what your god possesses?" I do not know the force of the Hebrew text: but I perceive that, in the Vulgate, Jephthah positively recognises the right of the god Chamos, and that the French translator weakened this admission by inserting an "according to you," which is not in the Latin.

[10] It is quite clear that the Phocian war, which was called "the Sacred War," was not a war of religion. Its object was the punishment of acts of sacrilege, and not the conquest of unbelievers.

Christian peoples. As the new idea of a kingdom of the other world could never have occurred to pagans, they always looked on the Christians as really rebels, who, while feigning to submit, were only waiting for the chance to make themselves independent and their masters, and to usurp by guile the authority they pretended in their weakness to respect. This was the cause of the persecutions.

What the pagans had feared took place. Then everything changed its aspect: the humble Christians changed their language, and soon this so-called kingdom of the other world turned, under a visible leader, into the most violent of earthly despotisms.

However, as there have always been a prince and civil laws, this double power and conflict of jurisdiction have made all good polity impossible in Christian States; and men have never succeeded in finding out whether they were bound to obey the master or the priest.

Several peoples, however, even in Europe and its neighbourhood, have desired without success to preserve or restore the old system: but the spirit of Christianity has everywhere prevailed. The sacred cult has always remained or again become independent of the Sovereign, and there has been no necessary link between it and the body of the State. Mahomet held very sane views, and linked his political system well together; and, as long as the form of his government continued under the caliphs who succeeded him, that government was indeed one, and so far good. But the Arabs, having grown prosperous, lettered, civilised, slack and cowardly, were conquered by barbarians: the division between the two powers began again; and, although it is less apparent among the Mahometans than among the Christians, it none the less exists, especially in the sect of Ali, and there are States, such as Persia, where it is continually making itself felt.

Among us, the Kings of England have made themselves heads of the Church, and the Czars have done the same: but this title has made them less its masters than its ministers; they have gained not so much the right to change it, as the power to maintain it: they are not its legislators, but only its princes. Wherever the clergy is a corporate body,[11] it is master and legislator in its own country. There are thus two powers, two Sovereigns, in England and in Russia, as well as elsewhere.

Of all Christian writers, the philosopher Hobbes alone has seen the evil and how to remedy it, and has dared to propose the reunion of the two heads of the eagle, and the restoration throughout of political unity, without which no State or government will ever be rightly constituted. But he should have seen that the masterful spirit of Christianity is incompatible with his system, and that the priestly interest would always be stronger than that of the State. It is not so much what is false and terrible in his political theory, as what is just and true, that has drawn down hatred on it.[12]

I believe that if the study of history were developed from this point of view, it would be easy to refute the contrary opinions of Bayle and Warburton, one of whom holds that religion can be of no use to the body politic, while the other, on the contrary, maintains that Christianity is its strongest support. We should demonstrate to the former that no

---

[11] It should be noted that the clergy find their bond of union not so much in formal assemblies, as in the communion of Churches. Communion and ex-communication are the social compact of the clergy, a compact which will always make them masters of peoples and kings. All priests who communicate together are fellow-citizens, even if they come from opposite ends of the earth. This invention is a masterpiece of statesmanship: there is nothing like it among pagan priests; who have therefore never formed a clerical corporate body.

[12] See, for instance, in a letter from Grotius to his brother (April 11, 1643), what that learned man found to praise and to blame in the *De Cive*. It is true that, with a bent for indulgence, he seems to pardon the writer the good for the sake of the bad; but all men are not so forgiving.

State has ever been founded without a religious basis, and to the latter, that the law of Christianity at bottom does more harm by weakening than good by strengthening the constitution of the State. To make myself understood, I have only to make a little more exact the too vague ideas of religion as relating to this subject.

Religion, considered in relation to society, which is either general or particular, may also be divided into two kinds: the religion of man, and that of the citizen. The first, which has neither temples, nor altars, nor rites, and is confined to the purely internal cult of the supreme God and the eternal obligations of morality, is the religion of the Gospel pure and simple, the true theism, what may be called natural divine right or law. The other, which is codified in a single country, gives it its gods, its own tutelary patrons; it has its dogmas, its rites, and its external cult prescribed by law; outside the single nation that follows it, all the world is in its sight infidel, foreign and barbarous; the duties and rights of man extend for it only as far as its own altars. Of this kind were all the religions of early peoples, which we may define as civil or positive divine right or law.

There is a third sort of religion of a more singular kind, which gives men two codes of legislation, two rulers, and two countries, renders them subject to contradictory duties, and makes it impossible for them to be faithful both to religion and to citizenship. Such are the religions of the Lamas and of the Japanese, and such is Roman Christianity, which may be called the religion of the priest. It leads to a sort of mixed and anti-social code which has no name.

In their political aspect, all these three kinds of religion have their defects. The third is so clearly bad, that it is waste of time to stop to prove it such. All that destroys social unity is worthless; all institutions that set man in contradiction to himself are worthless.

The second is good in that it unites the divine cult with love of the laws, and, making country the object of the citizens' adoration, teaches them that service done to the State is service done to its tutelary god. It is a form of theocracy, in which there can be no pontiff save the prince, and no priests save the magistrates. To die for one's country then becomes martyrdom; violation of its laws, impiety; and to subject one who is guilty to public execration is to condemn him to the anger of the gods: *Sacer estod.*

On the other hand, it is bad in that, being founded on lies and error, it deceives men, makes them credulous and superstitious, and drowns the true cult of the Divinity in empty ceremonial. It is bad, again, when it becomes tyrannous and exclusive, and makes a people bloodthirsty and intolerant, so that it breathes fire and slaughter, and regards as a sacred act the killing of every one who does not believe in its gods. The result is to place such a people in a natural state of war with all others, so that its security is deeply endangered.

There remains therefore the religion of man or Christianity—not the Christianity of to-day, but that of the Gospel, which is entirely different By means of this holy, sublime, and real religion all men, being children of one God, recognise one another as brothers, and the society that unites them is not dissolved even at death.

But this religion, having no particular relation to the body politic, leaves the laws in possession of the force they have in themselves without making any addition to it; and thus one of the great bonds that unite society considered in severalty fails to operate. Nay, more, so far from binding the hearts of the citizens to the State, it has the effect of taking them away from all earthly things. I know of nothing more contrary to the social spirit.

We are told that a people of true Christians would form the most perfect society imaginable. I see in this supposition only one great difficulty: that a society of true Christians would not be a society of men.

I say further that such a society, with all its perfection, would be neither the strongest nor the most lasting: the very fact that it was perfect would rob it of its bond of union; the flaw that would destroy it would lie in its very perfection.

Every one would do his duty; the people would be law-abiding, the rulers just and temperate; the magistrates upright and incorruptible; the soldiers would scorn death; there would be neither vanity nor luxury. So far, so good; but let us hear more.

Christianity as a religion is entirely spiritual, occupied solely with heavenly things; the country of the Christian is not of this world. He does his duty, indeed, but does it with profound indifference to the good or ill success of his cares. Provided he has nothing to reproach himself with, it matters little to him whether things go well or ill here on earth. If the State is prosperous, he hardly dares to share in the public happiness, for fear he may grow proud of his country's glory; if the State is languishing, he blesses the hand of God that is hard upon His people.

For the State to be peaceable and for harmony to be maintained, all the citizens without exception would have to be good Christians; if by ill hap there should be a single self-seeker or hypocrite, a Catiline or a Cromwell, for instance, he would certainly get the better of his pious compatriots. Christian charity does not readily allow a man to think hardly of his neighbours. As soon as, by some trick, he has discovered the art of imposing on them and getting hold of a share in the public authority, you have a man established in dignity; it is the will of God that he be respected: very soon you have a power; it is God's will that it be obeyed: and if the power is abused by him who wields it, it is the scourge wherewith God punishes His children. There would be scruples about driving out the usurper: public tranquillity would have to be disturbed, violence would have to be employed, and blood spilt; all this accords ill with Christian meekness; and after all, in this vale of sorrows, what does it matter whether we are free men or serfs? The essential thing is to get to heaven, and resignation is only an additional means of doing so.

If war breaks out with another State, the citizens march readily out to battle; not one of them thinks of flight; they do their duty, but they have no passion for victory; they know better how to die than how to conquer. What does it matter whether they win or lose? Does not Providence know better than they what is meet for them? Only think to what account a proud, impetuous and passionate enemy could turn their stoicism! Set over against them those generous peoples who were devoured by ardent love of glory and of their country, imagine your Christian republic face to face with Sparta or Rome: the pious Christians will be beaten, crushed and destroyed, before they know where they are, or will owe their safety only to the contempt their enemy will conceive for them. It was to my mind a fine oath that was taken by the soldiers of Fabius, who swore, not to conquer or die, but to come back victorious—and kept their oath. Christians, would never have taken such an oath; they would have looked on it as tempting God.

But I am mistaken in speaking of a Christian republic; the terms are mutually exclusive. Christianity preaches only servitude and dependence. Its spirit is so favourable to tyranny that it always profits by such a *régime*. True Christians are made to be slaves, and they know it and do not much mind: this short life counts for too little in their eyes.

I shall be told that Christian troops are excellent. I deny it. Show me an instance. For my part, I know of no Christian troops. I shall be told of the Crusades. Without disputing the valour of the Crusaders, I answer that, so far from being Christians, they were the priests' soldiery, citizens of the Church. They fought for their spiritual country, which the Church had, somehow or other, made temporal. Well understood, this goes back to paganism: as the Gospel sets up no national religion, a holy war is impossible among Christians.

Under the pagan emperors, the Christian soldiers were brave; every Christian writer affirms it, and I believe it: it was a case of honourable emulation of the pagan troops. As soon as the emperors were Christian, this emulation no longer existed, and, when the Cross had driven out the eagle, Roman valour wholly disappeared.

But, setting aside political considerations, let us come back to what is right, and settle our principles on this important point. The right which the social compact gives the Sovereign over the subjects does not, we have seen, exceed the limits of public expediency.[13] The subjects then owe the Sovereign an account of their opinions only to such an extent as they matter to the community. Now, it matters very much to the community that each citizen should have a religion. That will make him love his duty; but the dogmas of that religion concern the State and its members only so far as they have reference to morality and to the duties which he who professes them is bound to do to others. Each man may have, over and above, what opinions he pleases, without it being the Sovereign's business to take cognisance of them; for, as the Sovereign has no authority in the other world, whatever the lot of its subjects may be in the life to come, that is not its business, provided they are good citizens in this life.

There is therefore a purely civil profession of faith of which the Sovereign should fix the articles, not exactly as religious dogmas, but as social sentiments without which a man cannot be a good citizen or a faithful subject.[14] While it can compel no one to believe them, it can banish from the State whoever does not believe them—it can banish him, not for impiety, but as an anti-social being, incapable of truly loving the laws and justice, and of sacrificing, at need, his life to his duty. If any one, after publicly recognising these dogmas, behaves as if he does not believe them, let him be punished by death: he has committed the worst of all crimes, that of lying before the law.

The dogmas of civil religion ought to be few, simple, and exactly worded, without explanation or commentary. The existence of a mighty, intelligent and beneficent Divinity, possessed of foresight and providence, the life to come, the happiness of the just, the punishment of the wicked, the sanctity of the social contract and the laws: these are its positive dogmas. Its negative dogmas I confine to one, intolerance, which is a part of the cults we have rejected.

Those who distinguish civil from theological intolerance are, to my mind, mistaken. The two forms are inseparable. It is impossible to live at peace with those we regard as damned; to love them would be to hate God who punishes them: we positively must either reclaim or torment them. Wherever theological intolerance is admitted, it must inevitably have some civil effect;[15] and as soon as it has such an effect, the Sovereign is

---

[13] "In the republic," says the Marquis d'Argenson, "each man is perfectly free in what does not harm others." This is the invariable limitation, which it is impossible to define more exactly. I have not been able to deny myself the pleasure of occasionally quoting from this manuscript, though it is unknown to the public, in order to do honour to the memory of a good and illustrious man, who had kept even in the Ministry the heart of a good citizen, and views on the government of his country that were sane and right.

[14] Cæsar, pleading for Catiline, tried to establish the dogma that the soul is mortal: Cato and Cicero, in refutation, did not waste time in philosophising. They were content to show that Cæsar spoke like a bad citizen, and brought forward a doctrine that would have a bad effect on the State. This, in fact, and not a problem of theology, was what the Roman senate had to judge.

[15] Marriage, for instance, being a civil contract, has civil effects without which society cannot even subsist Suppose a body of clergy should claim the sole right of permitting this act, a right which every intolerant religion must of necessity claim, is it not clear that in establishing the authority of the Church in this respect, it will be destroying that of the prince, who will have thenceforth only as many subjects as the clergy choose to allow him? Being in a position to marry or not to marry people, according to their acceptance of such

no longer Sovereign even in the temporal sphere: thenceforth priests are the real masters, and kings only their ministers.

Now that there is and can be no longer an exclusive national religion, tolerance should be given to all religions that tolerate others, so long as their dogmas contain nothing contrary to the duties of citizenship. But whoever dares to say: *Outside the Church is no salvation,* ought to be driven from the State, unless the State is the Church, and the prince the pontiff. Such a dogma is good only in a theocratic government; in any other, it is fatal. The reason for which Henry IV is said to have embraced the Roman religion ought to make every honest man leave it, and still more any prince who knows how to reason.

CHAPTER IX: CONCLUSION

Now that I have laid down the true principles of political right, and tried to give the State a basis of its own to rest on, I ought next to strengthen it by its external relations, which would include the law of nations, commerce, the right of war and conquest, public right, leagues, negotiations, treaties, etc. But all this forms a new subject that is far too vast for my narrow scope. I ought throughout to have kept to a more limited sphere.

---

and such a doctrine, their admission or rejection of such and such a formula, their greater or less piety, the Church alone, by the exercise of prudence and firmness, will dispose of all inheritances, offices and citizens, and even of the State itself, which could not subsist if it were composed entirely of bastards? But, I shall be told, there will be appeals on the ground of abuse, summonses and decrees; the temporalities will be seized. How sad! The clergy, however little, I will not say courage, but sense it has, will take no notice and go its way: it will quietly allow appeals, summonses, decrees and seizures, and, in the end, will remain the master. It is not, I think, a great sacrifice to give up a part, when one is sure of securing all.

CPSIA information can be obtained
at www.ICGtesting.com
Printed in the USA
BVHW031027240121
598597BV00007B/176